America and East Asia

America and East Asia

A New Thirty Years War?

RICHARD HARRIS

GEORGE BRAZILLER • NEW YORK

For information address the publisher:
George Braziller, Inc.
One Park Avenue, New York, N.Y. 10016

FIRST PRINTING

Library of Congress Catalog Card Number 69-18078

Designed by Jennie Bush
Printed in the United States of America

Foreword to the American Edition

IN THE ENGLISH edition of this book I began the foreword by saying that more of the world's ills could be blamed on the war in Vietnam than on anything else. Despite the setback of the Russian invasion of Czechoslovakia, I think this is still true. However great the harm done by that invasion to international good faith, the Vietnam war still stands out as the biggest barrier to a detente between Russia and the United States. Only when that war has been settled can that detente move forward, even, one might hope, when Russian suspicions are allayed, to the point of encouraging a new Russian attitude to eastern Europe that could unlock the tensions which sent half a million troops into Czechoslovakia last August.

Nor is it only the prospects of world peace that are marred by the Vietnam war. Lately, economists have pointed to the war as the biggest single cause of the world's monetary disequilibrium, leading to the gold crisis of early 1968. If a balance sheet is struck, a whole host of political and economic difficulties, over and above the suffering of those directly involved in Vietnam, can be charged to this war.

In this foreword to the American edition of this book I hardly need to stress those aspects of the war that have struck home hardest in the United States. The losses in men killed and wounded have now reached a heavy total. The longer the war has gone on the more America has been divided by it. It has been an issue in the forefront of the revolution on all university campuses. Almost a quarter of a century after the end of World War II it is the Vietnam war that makes people everywhere feel that war is intolerable.

This sense of revulsion against the war has been emphasized by the war's public character. The war in Vietnam is the first television war, watched on their screens by hundreds of millions of people every week for three years or more, read about in newspapers, seen in films. All the time there is the instant portrayal and the instant horror.

There are those who find it possible to give unqualified support to one side or the other in this war and thus to look for the victory of one side without much reference to the cost of that victory. However, more and more protest at the war—not least in the United States itself—has expressed a revulsion against the belief that any worthwhile ends can come from such means.

Vietnam became a major issue in the recent presidential election, and it will be a major concern for President Nixon when he takes office. A start has been made on peace negotiations, and there are hopes that they will lead to some settlement before 1969 ends. But when that happens American involvement with East Asia will not have ended and it is this wider subject that concerns me. So this is not a book about the Vietnam war, though it springs from it. It began as three articles published in *The Times* (London) in February, 1968. The aim of the articles was to put the Vietnam war in a context different from those in which it is commonly seen. Not a cold war context, though that cannot be ignored; nor that of an isolated war, which it is not. I wanted to give this war the perspective of the civilization to which Vietnam belongs and of the wider and no less historical confrontation in which the United States is involved and of which this war is the outcome.

Any attempt to outline the shape of historical events necessarily means making sharp edges where they do not exist; the ideas in the minds of all the actors in this drama do not accord with the attitudes which I have attributed to both China and the United States in what follows. Moreover, the confrontation which I have picked out and emphasized is not meant to reject all the other arguments, political or economic, national or international, which affect the Vietnam war. I am concerned only with putting this war in a new perspective, one which I think is more important and possibly more revealing than those common to newspapers or politicians.

The ideas set forth in this book—much expanded from the three original articles—first took shape in my mind when I spent the years 1947 to 1950 in China, seeing the downfall of the Kuomintang government and watching the first year of Communist rule. Thereafter, as *The Times* correspondent in Hongkong and in Singapore, I continued to follow events in China but also visited Vietnam and other parts of Southeast Asia. It was then that I was forcibly struck by those characteristics of a common civilization shared by both China and Vietnam—

and especially manifest in their Communist régimes—which marked out this area of civilization from the rest of Asia. As my acquaintance with the whole continent of Asia grew in travels throughout the 1950's I became more and more convinced that the cultural character of all these countries would matter more in the long run than the influences which were attributed to nationalism, anticolonialism or Western-imported ideologies whether specifically Communist or vaguely socialist, important as these might seem. These ideas have played and still play their part; what matters is that they must be seen at work in the context of each civilization.

First, then, a definition of the civilization. Geographical terms can sometimes be disastrous. Asia—in itself a European definition as a geographical term—can at least be simplified by sharply marking off from the rest the one civilization which preserves its distinctive character and which retains a unity that the rest lacks—East Asia. In South Asia, Hindu, Muslim, and Buddhist cultures exist like a layer cake; only in East Asia has a continuous growth evolved a powerfully knit set of ideas common to all its constituent parts—China, Japan, Korea, and Vietnam. In using the term East Asia I mean a civilization, as one thinks of Europe as a civilization, and not a geographical area.

Certainly Southeast Asia has been the most flabby geographical bundle to have been introduced into the world's strategic and political thinking. It is a fiction. To include Vietnam within it is to start from an entirely false assumption that invalidates almost all the rest. Of all the troubled areas of the world in which Western intervention of some kind has tried to bring "security" or "stability," Vietnam is the worst case of ignorance.

Ignorance, that is to say, of the possibilities derived from the history and culture which makes one country in Asia quite different from another.

Everyone must hope that a settlement will be reached in Vietnam. But even if it removes the worst sore in the world at this moment it will not have ended the conflict I have tried to sketch in these pages. Vietnam has been so much in the front of our minds that the other elements of the East Asian confrontation with the United States, China especially, have receded into the background. The Pueblo incident was a reminder that tensions could once again come to the surface in Korea. On the other hand China's absorption in the cultural revolution, and the chance whereby Mao Tse-tung's fiercest venom has lately been directed against the Russians, has made many people forget how much remains to be solved between China and America. The roots of the war in Vietnam are there.

This essay attempts to expose all these roots by going back in history. It is written looking out from China, as it were, and this will be thought to be a bias. I do not apologize for the bias. Almost all the books written about Asia, and especially those written about Southeast Asia, tend to look from the rim inward at the vast and very much unknown—and therefore the more feared—mass of China. These fears have taken some alarming shapes since the People's government won power in 1949. Many charges can be made against that government, most of all in its international behavior. China can reply with a long list of charges, too, and many of them are just. But whatever out opinions we shall never be on terms with China until we understand its nature and outlook—both have been evolving for a very long time.

When historians come to look back on the twentieth century they may describe its major international confrontation not as the one between the "third world" and the rest—the rich and the poor; not even, perhaps, between the white and colored races, since there are so many differences within each grouping, but between East Asia and the rest of the world. And so in taking as my framework the confrontation between East Asia and the United States I should not be taken to exclude the importance of the wider confrontation. No other countries have really understood the nature of East Asia. No other countries have solved their relationship with the new China to their satisfaction. It is because for nearly twenty years now the United States has been at war with one or other part of this civilization and may find itself grappling for another decade that it forms the subject of this book.

My analysis of American attitudes is not based on as much knowledge of the United States as a civilization as I would wish. But I have, in a childhood spent in China, and since then in the Second World War and in the postwar decades, had much opportunity of observing Americans in China and around its periphery in East Asia. As a newspaper correspondent I was able to observe the attitudes toward China and to see how common was the emotional attachment of Americans irrespective of their political affiliations. And these emotions were concentrated on China to the exclusion of all other parts of Asia with which the American connection had been historically slender.

The subject matter of this book will not, however, last forever. Indeed, one might claim that the era of American confrontation with East Asia is now coming to its end. It will never again be a relationship as singular or as committed as it was during the decades when this area alone was the area on which American national emotions were fixed. In one sense, of course, there will always be a close involvement on account of geography alone. But now that America is a world power, worldwide interests will slowly reduce East Asia to its proper place in the American world view. This adjustment will be easier and the disengagement more peaceful if the character of the confrontation and the nature of East Asian civilization are better understood than they have been since World War II. This book attempts to offer some clues to a better understanding of the confrontation.

Contents

Maps

America and East Asia

Introduction

THE AGE CALLED by an Indian historian the Age of Vasco da Gama came to an end after the last war. The age of European expansion has been followed by imperial withdrawal. For a quarter of a century since World War II, the dismantling of European empire has created a succession of new nation states, all eagerly equipping themselves with the trappings of sovereignty and measuring themselves against their onetime Western rulers. Success or failure has usually meant economic success since this was a measure of the equality they sought as well as being the deficiency most often brought home to them in their relations with the West.

Thus the first postwar division of the world, the cold war division between the Communist world and what the Americans especially like to call the "free world," is being replaced by another division, the even more significant, because it is longer-lasting, division between the Western or developed world and the poorer, new, or under-developed nations.

These divisions are not only dangerously oversimplified and obsessed by quantitative economic criteria; they are, for most of the countries of Asia, based on Western ignorance of their history and culture. It is true that for some new countries in Africa that are themselves almost a creation of the imperial era, history and cultural traditions play a smaller part. And it is true also of a country like China, that enough is known in a vague kind of way of its history and culture so that even prime ministers in the West are capable of distinguishing by means other than size between Chad and China. But these attitudes still fall far short of the only really valid standpoint in judging any country: to look at what is happening now as an outgrowth from its past as well as from the impact of present events upon it; to give weight to all those factors that are just as important as economic data in the lives of these peoples; to see what social, religious, magical, traditional, literary, artistic, historical beliefs and traditions exist and still form the outlook of the society. Generalizations about the developing world, or about something which we in the West have called "Asia"—the Chinese had no word for Asia and have simply adopted the European usage—will only confuse us. The divisions in the world that matter are those between zones of different civilizations where language, religion, shared historical experience, such as alien conquest, climate, and geographic as well as economic factors, have gone to the making of the present. When we say Europe we mean a civilization in this sense. When we divide it roughly into western and eastern Europe, we are also thinking of a historical and cultural division albeit blurred, and in using the expression we naturally reflect how much the past in eastern and western Europe goes to the making of the political division we know in the present.

The expansion of Europe in the age that began with the voyage of Vasco da Gama in 1498 took European power to the Americas, Asia, and Africa. In the Americas—broadly—native populations were evicted or suppressed to make way for incoming settlers; in Africa, historical traditions were not ancient or so well developed culturally as to revert to their old political pattern after the end of the colonial era; only in Asia do cultures exist with such traditions that are again making themselves felt after the suppressive tendencies as well as the innovations of an age of imperial rule.

In describing the subject matter of this book as the confrontation between America and East Asia, it would be interesting and relevant to draw the parallel between other confrontations of European countries and the Asian cultures over which they ruled in the imperial era. The basic character of mutual response and mutual reaction was much the same in these instances as in the one I analyze. As yet, historians have not made comparative studies of the confrontations of Western imperialism, though time will show which of the ruling countries has left the most lasting legacy in each Asian country. Britain, France, and Holland each faced very different cultures in those parts of Asia that they ruled. All kinds of national and cultural characteristics came into play on both sides. British reactions tended to be different as between Muslims and Hindus in India—would the French have been different if they had ruled India? What different results might have followed if Indonesia had been ruled by the British and Burma by the Dutch? In all these cases a two-way traffic existed: to explore the nature of imperialism in the abstract misses most of the subtleties of these confrontations. We must take each culture and observe it against the culture which had the impact.

The fact that the United States has not, in East Asia, been an imperial ruler or aspired to be one does not alter the character of the confrontation; it only limits its area of operation. The exertion of power, the emergence of hopes and expectations, the emotional commitment of one kind or another, these have been common to all Western countries in their involvement with Asia whether or not the involvement comprised imperial rule.

But to return to Vietnam, the starting point of this book. To understand Vietnam today, as understanding any other of the new nation states of Asia, we need to know roughly how things stood when the power of the West first made itself felt, how Western power was itself exerted to change the life of such a culture, and how both these factors face the new influences of the postwar world. To ask the question what happened? and how did it happen? can go quite a bit of the way to explain the reasons for what is now happening in Vietnam. And it can go a long way to reduce ignorant fears.

The Asian culture zone which is legitimately called "East Asia," using the term to define a civilization rather than to indicate a mere geographical area, largely escaped Western imperial rule, but the impact of the Western world was profound, and unlike the experience of the rest of Asia it was both European and American. My theme in this essay is the conflict between East Asia and America, two of the world's civilizations which I attempt to isolate because of their special character. My argument is that this conflict gains its special character from the nature of these two civilizations and the phase in their history through which each is passing. America is involved in conflict elsewhere—confronted by Cuba's communism and by Communist-led incipient guerrilla movements in many other places. China, too, during this last phase of Mao Tse-tung's revolutionary career, proclaims herself as the leader of such revolutions—always presupposing that Maoist philosophies of revolution are being followed. It would not be true to say that China leads these revolutions, to do so would in itself be contrary to Maoist revolutionary ideas. It is doubtful if China's aid amounts to very much. It will be one of my conclusions at the end of this analysis of East Asian characteristics that China's *outgoing* power, quite apart from China's intentions, is absurdly exaggerated in the Western world and in the rest of Asia as well.

But, whatever America is doing anywhere else in the world, and whatever causes China may be championing or whatever battles she fights against the Soviet "revisionists" and their lackeys fall outside my theme. I single out this conflict between America and East Asia because I think it best explains what has happened in the last twenty years in the Far East and what now concerns us all—Vietnam.

The war in Vietnam is part of one war, the bloodiest and most tenaciously fought part, that already has been going on for twenty years and may go on even more catastrophically if its true context is not seen for what it is. It would be natural to object that the ideological character on which I lay so much emphasis is also present, say, in the American confrontation with Cuba, not least with the confrontation with Russia and eastern Europe where the cold war began. To consider each of these cases separately would lead me too far from my main theme. Nevertheless, some brief reference should be made to Russia as the world's first and leading Communist state. Is the ideological determination not as great in this case as I claim it is in the conflict with East Asia? To argue this point at length, distinguishing the roots of communism in Russia from those in China, would take too much space. Suffice it to say that Russia, as a Communist country, is not inherently or historically or traditionally such a civilization. Certainly it has in the past been authoritarian, and this characteristic lives on. Certainly for all the revisionism or evolution we may expect to see in Russia and eastern Europe in the next half century there will be a residual element derived from Communist doctrine. But I would question whether Russia has been in the past or is now an ideological civilization of the kind that East Asia and the United States are even though, while Communist doctrine is predominant, it has the same character superficially.

1

Conflict Between the World's Two Ideological Civilizations

AN IDEOLOGICAL CIVILIZATION is taken to mean an area throughout which government is conducted in accordance with a particular set of beliefs about the nature of man and society, beliefs whose truth is thought by the rulers of that society to be both rational and self-evident. As a consequence, these truths are upheld by those rulers—and this will apply even if the society is democratic and not authoritarian, since by definition all political parties within the society share the basic beliefs. Hence, any challenge to the beliefs is taken to be a challenge to the society.

Within the society such ideological beliefs take precedence over any other beliefs of an other-worldly or religious character. Where such beliefs exist they are expected to sustain the prevalent, official doctrine. Thus, in the United States Christian churches have tended to exist in support rather than in opposition to what is felt to be the doctrine that sustains American society. So in China under Communist rule religious or other sects are expected to give their first allegiance to the doctrine of the state. The cases are not parallel, of course, but the assumptions that lie behind them are not far different.

In such ideological civilizations the moral basis of the state doctrine is paramount. If it should be questioned the intent is either mistaken or evil; if the doctrine is challenged outright then the intent is by definition evil. By contrast the adoption of the doctrine elsewhere, or any evidence of tribute paid to its moral superiority, is thought to be desirable and to be encouraged.

The clash between these two civilizations of East Asia and America has come about in this century because only then did the confrontation come about. It was a confrontation in the making during the first and second world wars which might almost be regarded in this context of civilizations as Europe's civil wars, but unlike either of these wars this is not a conflict within a civilization: the creeds at issue, the way of life expounded, belong to two separate and seemingly opposed traditions. One doctrine is fighting another doctrine.

It is undeniable that the conflict in Europe in which the United States plays a dominant part has also been posed in ideological terms. Containing Russia has meant to Americans containing communism even if for the rest of Europe the matter is not quite so simple as all that. Equally containing China might seem just another case of containing communism, but here too the background shows that there is more to it than the purely ideological issue. On the other hand it is plain that as time passes the confrontation of Russia and the United States becomes more and more a confrontation of powers, each calculating their offensive and defensive strength, and much less the kind of ideological battle that we see in

East Asia. The missiles and antimissiles, the spy trawlers and early warning systems, the hot lines, all go to show how advanced technology imposes its own structuralism, draining the confrontation of its ideology. It should be remembered that in Russia and eastern Europe communism is an intrusion into an existing society where religions and other beliefs are formally embodied in institutions. It is a revolutionary movement that seeks to overthrow or modify these institutions. In China this was not so. In this century all China has sought revolutionary change. The strongest impulses in society were in favor of the overthrow of existing institutions. The desire for a new China was unquestioned. Suffice it to say that the roots of the ideological character of East Asia are longer and far deeper than is communism in Russia and the very context in which communism exists in eastern Europe exposes it to a host of other and no less strongly held ideals about the nature of man and systems of government: all the time the total doctrine is being sapped by the influence of pragmatic thinking.

In East Asia, therefore, the conflict within each society has a different character. Its nature derives from the history and present renewal of East Asian civilization. To define that civilization one might take an arbitrary point at which the ideological character was first fixed. As good a turning point as any was when Wu Ti (140–87 B.C.), emperor of the Han dynasty, made examination in a set of beliefs about man and his obligations in society a necessity for entering public service. The changes in Chinese society at that time made the higher ranks of the bureaucracy the most prized positions in the state, and the examination system necessarily gave to office-holders a vested interest in the doctrines of which they had become the scholars and upholders. At that time Confucianism had already picked up extraneous wrappings and emendations; much more absorption and domestication of other ideas was to go into the Chinese melting pot over two millennia; but broadly these doctrines given the label of Confucianism have been the thread running through Chinese history and dominating most of the imperial dynasties. Hence, China's institutions, its political thinking, and the structure of its society have been profoundly influenced by an authoritarianism that offered no room for democracy but was at its best humane, believing that the natural goodness in man could be encouraged by good government, which essentially meant good men governing in accordance with good doctrine.

The other states that drew their ideological ways from the parent culture of China—though in different degrees —were Korea, Vietnam (both of which were ruled at some periods by China and remained vassals of a kind almost into this century), and Japan. Japan was never ruled by China nor acknowledged itself to be a vassal, but it is still a country on which the Chinese imprint has been profound and nowhere so profound as in the ideological conditioning of Japanese society and the political behavior that derives from it.

It must be added that for all three of these countries China was the source of a classical tradition almost exactly as Greece and Rome have been such a source for all Europe. Classical Chinese was as much the necessary equipment of a scholar in Korea, Vietnam, or Japan as Greek and Latin were the foundations of scholarship in Europe. The philosophers of China and especially the classical texts associated with Confucianism were as much a subject of study as Greek and Latin authors have been in the universities of Europe. Moreover, the Chinese written language, in itself unique, remains to this day the written form for ordinary Japanese, is in common and partial use in Korea, and remained until a generation ago the natural equipment of the scholar in Vietnam even though as a written form for the Vietnamese language it was gradually displaced by the romanized form devised by the Jesuit missionary Alexandre de Rhodes in the seventeenth century and popularized under French rule two centuries later to the eventual exclusion of the Chinese characters.

To Europeans who think immediately of church and state it should be added that religion in this civilization—chiefly Buddhism in its variants—never set up the hierarchy of a separate power. Often a solace for privacy, a resort for the illiterate (in a society where literacy more than anything defined class), or a useful ritual to accompany ceremonies of birth and death, it never acquired the organization of a church in the European sense. The state was all and the proper ordering of society on this earth was the normal task of the upright man.

Of course there are important differences between the component parts of this civilization, between Japan and China especially, differences every bit as great as between Spain and Germany or Denmark and Italy: but so are the similarities as great as those that have made Europe what it is. In any case, the point that is being made here and that is relevant to this seemingly insoluble conflict is the political character of East Asian civilization and its norms of political behavior, the one thing more than anything else that links these countries. How political man thinks and behaves in East Asia is what concerns us.

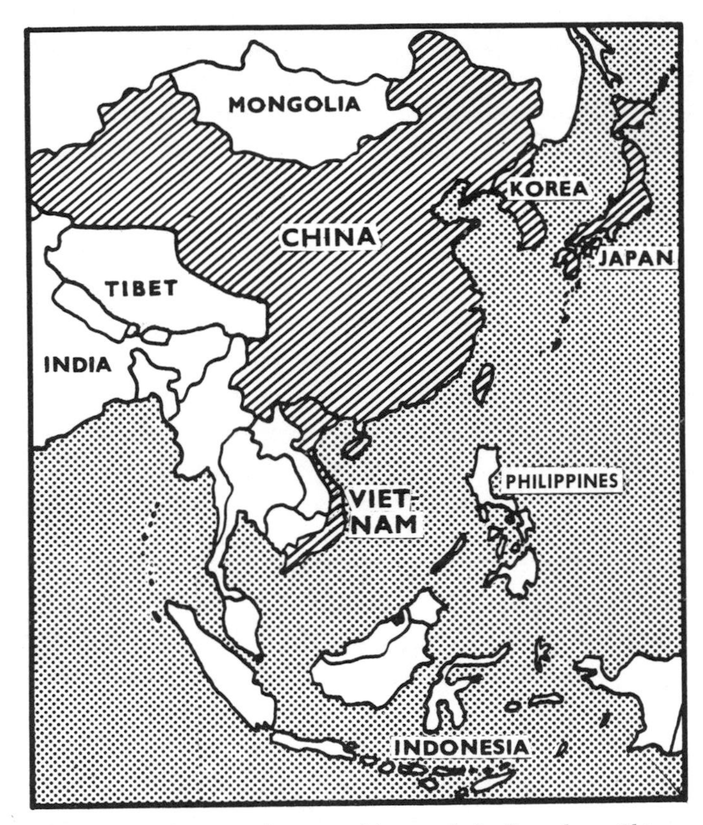

MAP 1. East Asian civilization. (Areas of shading show Chinese cultural area.) The historical and cultural links that bind China, Japan, Korea, and Vietnam into one civilization are as close and extend as far back in time as those that have made Europe what it is. For all of these countries Chinese has been the classical language and Chinese characters have provided the written form of their own language. Chinese philosophy has been the natural study of the educated man. Chinese culture has been imported and imitated. Above all the ideas that governed the Confucian political system have formed the political thinking and the world view of this area.

Of course, the degrees of this influence vary. Japan is by far the most independent, never having been a vassal of China and evolving in its own way both in culture and religion. Korea and Vietnam, on the other hand, have been either directly ruled by

It was only in the nineteenth century that the contact of Europe and the United States on this civilization forced it to change. Before that it had lived in its own world system, a system in which China was the center (*Chung Kuo*: the central or middle Kingdom) and the rest—in theory—tributaries (see map on p. 14). Change was forced upon all the component parts of East Asia during the nineteenth century. In China the upheaval has been greatest. All the other countries have changed too. Japan went about it in its own way. Korea was brought under Japanese rule and was changed by Japan. Vietnam was the only part of the East Asian zone to be brought under European colonial rule.

At the core of this process of change was the necessity of rejecting the old doctrine of the state and the consequent need for its replacement by a new doctrine that served the national purpose, that is to say to serve as a foundation within the society while also seeming to meet the demands of the wider world into which East Asia was being drawn.

But in taking this step of renewal, in substituting a new doctrine for the old, there was no change in the old habits. Communism in China, Korea, and Vietnam carries on the old sense of self-righteousness while remaking the doctrine into forms adapted to national needs. China's belief in her ancient superiority is just as strong

---

China or been close Chinese vassals for most of their existence. On both, the Chinese stamp remains profound. Only Vietnam has been brought under the colonial rule of a European power, France, for less than a century, though the influence of the Roman Catholic religion extends back for more than two centuries and is a factor in Vietnam as it is not in any other East Asian country.

East Asia is the one part of the continent we in the West have called "Asia" that forms a distinct civilization and has maintained that coherence in the face of Western influence.

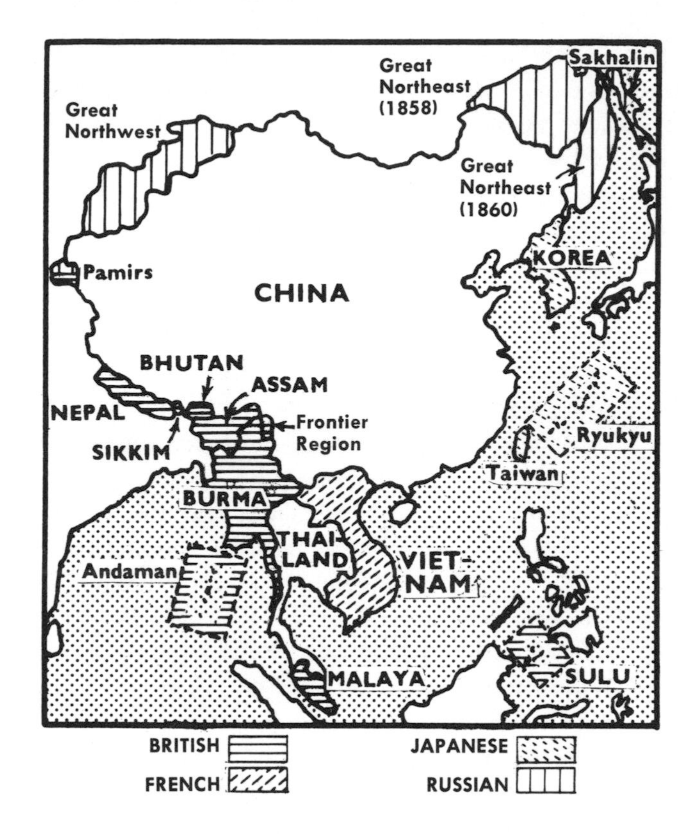

MAP 2. The Chinese Empire and the Chinese world. This map was published in a book in Communist China. It expresses the generalized sense of resentment that all Chinese feel at the loss of territory and influence during a century of Western incursion and Chinese weakness. In fact, this map shows two quite separate things. There are the cessions of territory that were at the time under Chinese rule—mostly in the eastern maritime territories of Siberia and in central Asia. Also, the peripheral zones of Chinese authority which became autonomous or were under some foreign influence—Manchuria, Sinkiang, Tibet (they are not separately marked on this map). Second, there are the territories that were independently ruled but which paid tribute to the Chinese Emperor and formed part of what then seemed to the Chinese a working world system of which they were the center and natural apex.

today under the new doctrine. The old conviction and dedication have a new creed to cling to, a creed that rejects their molesters of the past century as imperialists. The moral foundations of East Asia are now thought to have been put back on a higher pedestal from which the Western invasion can be thrown back.

It will be obvious that one of the four East Asian countries—Japan—has not yet fallen within this pattern. Japan's renewal was conducted in a different way. The reformers of the late nineteenth century were more ready than were the Chinese to throw over Confucianism. The structure of Japanese society also enabled entrepreneurs to emerge more easily than in China and thus to set Japan on a course of economic development that now astounds the world. While China first struggled to find a doctrine and on it to rebuild the state, Japan was happy to modernize herself economically and militarily. What Japan has not yet done is to find a doctrine to serve as the moral foundation of its new society, though the desire for such a doctrine still manifests itself in many ways. Nationalism—of a spurious kind—was inflated into such a doctrine before the war and then failed.

Some would argue that Japan's recent development is at a tangent, removing it from the old pull of East Asia. Against this it can be said that Japan's political thinking

---

In assessing Chinese behavior today it is useful to recall this old world—(after all, it is not so far removed in time; its last gasp might be defined as the final journey of a tributary mission from Nepal as late as 1908) which influences Chinese thinking while she is adjusting herself to a new world.

The main outstanding issue is the return to mainland rule of Taiwan; Hongkong and Macao are secondary questions in Chinese thinking. The territories ceded to Russia, while a useful weapon with which to lash revisionists, are unlikely to be made a serious territorial claim; these areas became part of China only by virtue of the Manchu conquest in the seventeenth century.

and behavior is as much ideological as it ever was and that the habits brought about by Confucianism are still visible—the impulse toward conformity, for example, or the lack of an individual identity and a desire for individual choice that are the essence of democracy as we know it—Japan is not now part of the confrontation and can best be left out of this analysis. The example of Japan is, nevertheless, not—or not yet—evidence to refute the basic argument put forward in this essay. Could it be that Japan's lack of a doctrine explains Japan's international uncertainty, torn between East Asian affiliations and her alliance with the United States, for all the power that an advanced economy gives? Is economic power, one might almost ask, a valid form of power to the East Asian mind? These are questions that may not be answered for a half a century. Japan for the present must be set aside.

THE AMERICAN WAY OF THOUGHT

So much for the first of the contestants—East Asia. Much less explanation is needed to define the other ideological civilization that now finds itself at war with East Asia. In the United States the rational and self-evident truths on which society should be ordered were set forth long after the Han dynasty—on July 4, 1776. By this formal gesture of independence, the United States turned its back on Europe politically and consciously laid new political foundations.

Max Lerner in *America as a Civilization* writes of "the psychic necessity for rejecting Europe that has affected the whole spectrum of American social thinking" and notes how the American is led to reject ideas for social change because they are European and Marxist. "In his spiritual isolation the middle class American seems to suffer from a sense of encirclement and to identify with a 'European' or 'foreign' source whatever ills he feels he is subject to."

These new political foundations were felt to be morally superior to the societies that had been left behind—as indeed they were—and consequently there grew up the attitude that what had been rejected—"the slaying of the European father" is Max Lerner's phrase —was a Europe complacent and lacking in a real love of liberty. An illustration of this attitude in a somewhat extreme form can be taken from the occasion during the Second World War when American troops were about to make the first assault in Europe in the Sicily landing of July, 1943, General Patton, their commander, issued an order:

> When we land we will meet German and Italian soldiers whom it is our honor and privilege to attack and destroy. Many of you have in your veins German and Italian blood, but remember that these ancestors of yours so loved freedom that they gave up home and country to cross the ocean in search of liberty. The ancestors of the people we shall kill lacked the courage to make such a sacrifice and continued as slaves.*

Much more consciously, with much greater speed, and with the working out over the past century of effective methods of indoctrination of immigrants, the United States has come to adopt the same attitude that China, instinctively and over a much longer period has adopted: it has assumed that those who did not share its enlighten-

* Quoted in Geoffrey Gorer, *The Americans* (London: Cresset Press, 1948), p. 13.

ment were unfortunate, that those who came to live within its society must be instructed in the doctrine and must live by its rules, and that those who questioned the doctrine were evil or misguided.

Evidence of the doctrinal character of Americanism—to match the word to Confucianism—is so plentiful that a few quotations will suffice. Engraved on the Statue of Liberty, the doctrine was the first thing to meet the immigrant. In every important political speech echoes of the founding fathers abound. This, for instance:

> Our destiny in the midst of change will rest on the unchanged character of our people—and on their faith. They came here—the exile and the stranger, brave and frightened—to find a place where a man could be his own man. They made a covenant with this land. Conceived in justice, written in liberty, bound in union, it was meant one day to inspire the hopes of all mankind. It binds us still. And if we keep its terms we shall flourish.

The words could have come from almost any speech of this century. In fact the extract comes from President Johnson's inaugural address of January, 1965, in which all the central themes of Americanism are reiterated. Most relevant to the struggle now in progress with East Asia is the worldwide ambition:

> The American covenant called on us to help show the way for the liberation of man. That is still our goal. Thus, if as a nation there is much outside our control, as a people no stranger is outside our hope . . . dangers and troubles we once called "foreign" now live among us. If American lives must end, and American treasure be spilled, in countries we barely know, that is the price that change has demanded of conviction.

Or at quite a different level, but in its way no less revealing, there are the words in which the president of the Dow Chemical Company justifies one of his products: "We believe," he is reported as saying in defense of his company's manufacture of napalm, "in fulfilling our responsibility to this national commitment of a democratic society." The ideological thinking could hardly be more explicit.

A perceptive critic of American ideological conviction, the poet Robert Lowell, comments: "Our world position is a curious sort of fulfillment of a national characteristic: that we're a country founded on a constitution. That makes us rather different from the usual country founded on a history and a culture. We were founded on a Declaration, on the Constitution, on Principles, and we've always had the idea of 'saving the world.' And that comes close to perhaps destroying the world. Suddenly it is as though this really terrible nightmare has come true, that we are suddenly in a position where we might destroy the world, and that is very closely allied to saving it." It is one of the great virtues of America that it has never lacked critics of its received faith when it seems to be put to mistaken uses. Robert Lowell is one such. From the heart of the American political system a critic can also speak. "The problem of excessive ideological zeal," Senator Fulbright has said, "is our own problem as well as the Communists'."

Both these ideological civilizations express their political ambitions in different ways in different parts of the world. To the United States communism is the enemy wherever it may spring up because it is liable to undermine the ideology of Americanism. But the involvement of either China or the United States in the affairs of other parts of the world is incidental if not peripheral to my theme: this theme is the special character of the involvement between China (and thus by necessary connection East Asian civilization) and the United States. It is this special character of a mutual involvement that determines what has happened on this Pacific front in the past twenty years, this special character that fuels the emotions of the war in Vietnam.

In the war in which these two ideological civilizations are locked each has its charges against the other. Aggression, expansion, imperialism—the words fly back and forth. But it is not necessarily in the nature of either of these civilizations deliberately to foment the conflict that has come about. History, geography, chance of various kinds, set the scene in ways that neither combatant foresaw at the time. Let us follow its course from the beginning.

2

How the Confrontation Came About

HOW HAS THE confrontation between East Asia and the United States come about? Why does America now find itself hacking vainly at the tough fiber of East Asia at ever greater cost in men and money? The war in Vietnam has done more to damage American reputation in the world than anything else since the full force of the United States as a world power sprung armed from the Second World War. Can we blame simply President Johnson's lack of vision? Alternatively is the tragedy of Vietnam to be explained merely by Ho Chi Minh's intransigent nationalism to which the United States is responding in the only way it could? Is the battle today only between the wills of these two men and does all the suffering hang on that?

Of course, the war can be ended by negotiations and can only be ended in this way. This is the immediate and urgent need. But it is not my purpose to sketch the possible terms of a settlement, so much as to define the historical and ideological conditions that must inescapably govern such a settlement. Yet an essay of this kind cannot avoid some blame by implication even if any attempt to present a balance sheet is rejected. The blame for war in Vietnam goes right back to the last years of the war and the period immediately afterward. French action in 1945 and British action in aid of the French at that time all comes into it. Inevitably, since this essay deals with the confrontation of East Asia and America, it is American errors that will tend to stand out rather than the actions of European imperial powers in the closing days of empire. Of course, President Johnson has his own errors to look back on, and before that the errors of Kennedy and Eisenhower and Truman—even Roosevelt—must all be brought into the balance if we are considering only Vietnam. But Vietnam is only part of the whole East Asian scene, only the latest act of this tragedy that begins to seem in its pointless destruction like another Thirty Years War. It is the roots of this confrontation that I want to expose; the elements in the tragedy that I want to lay bare. And the truth is that this confrontation goes much further back into the texture of history, where blame is a thread lost in the general pattern.

While this essay deals only with the confrontation of America and East Asia, there is a larger, and let us hope less tragic confrontation, in which all of us are involved. That is the confrontation between East Asia and the world as a whole. This civilization, which developed in one area of the world and has evolved for three thousand years in that area, has only in the last century had to face the outside world and adjust its enclosed and private ways to those of assertive outsiders. Some of the interesting complications in this process are geographical. What we have in the case of China, for example, is the conflict between a land-based power and the power of expansionist Europeans whose spirit and impetus came from crossing the seas in eager pursuit of trade and fired by curiosity. Portugal, Spain, Britain, Holland, and France were all such maritime powers.

It is worth noting that in modern times, from the age of Vasco da Gama onward, all western European contact with East Asian civilization has been made by sea. How much better an understanding of China must have been gained by those who made their way to China not through the Indian Ocean, touching on the exotic shores of the Coromandel Coast or Sumatra, but, like Marco Polo, pressed on day after weary day across the inhospitable plateaus of central Asia to debouch at last into the loess hills of northwest China. The Russians, too, with their missions in the seventeenth and eighteenth centuries were themselves a land-thinking power making a landward way to another land-thinking power. The geography matters.

In the confrontation of East Asia and America one should also start with geography. In the nineteenth century two things happened on each side of the Pacific. The United States grew as a nation to stand on the Pacific seaboard and to found its economic power. China, occupying a homeland unchanged throughout its history, slowly reacted to its own internal collapse and to the steady intrusion of Western power by finding in nationalism and in doctrine to back it the fuel of its renewal as an independent civilization. These two happenings were on either side of the Pacific. Geography alone seemed certain to bring these two ideological civilizations together in a century when the world was being made one. If, by contrast, the United States had faced not East Asia but the other Asian lands bordering the Indian Ocean the story would have been entirely different, for none of these are ideological civilizations of the East Asian type.

AMERICAN PROBING

Even before the Pacific coastline had come to play a part in American maritime history American ships began their trade with China. They were already in competition with the British and other European traders in the 1780's and 1790's as soon as American independence had become an established fact. Then came the renewed growth of the trade after 1820. At that time it was a neutral, commercial enterprise in which the Americans were happy to allow more thrusting European powers led by Britain to batter at the resisting walls of East Asia. Not that the Americans did not soon try this operation for themselves, sending a naval commodore to test Japan in 1846. He was insultingly repulsed. And after Britain's blasting of an entry in the Opium War the Americans were ready to follow in asking the Chinese to sign on the dotted line of their own trade treaty, backing up the demand with a naval squadron.

Further American probes toward Japan led to Commodore Perry's successful and forceful expedition in 1854, and this time it was the British who profited from the American initiative. Then came the further attempts by Britain and France from 1856 to 1860 to force China out of its old world and to make of her an inhabitant of the new world created by European expansion.

Certainly Perry's tactics had seemed the right ones to use in Japan, though the result was that Japan's own self-renewal began within a decade of his arrival. The restoration of the emperor Meiji began a course of disciplined self-renewal and successful modernization for the Japanese whose centenary is being celebrated this year. If imitation of the West and the rejection of Confucianism was the answer, Japan was ruthless enough to set about it. The tradition of borrowing from other countries was a strong one in any case. China, however, was not prepared thus to imitate the West. Chinese pride was too great. China resisted. Yet as the century ran on and the United States matured as a civilization, the special relationship between these two countries began to grow, though at first much more from the American side than from the Chinese.

The American policy that evolved in the twenty years following the Anglo-Chinese war of 1840 was to prevent any one European power from dominating China. This policy took formal shape only in 1899, with Secretary Hay's proclamation of the "Open Door" policy. Nevertheless, from the 1860's onward a particular and special relationship began to develop between America and China.

What happened was that the Americans began gradually to find in China a natural and desirable field for their endeavor. This was a country that needed aid and teaching; that needed hope and beliefs to rescue it from its downward spiral. What was more China looked like she was escaping from the European imperial rule that had been fastened on India, on Indonesia and that spread all through Southeast Asia—save for Thailand—by the end of the century.

China was too big, perhaps, certainly too proud, and perhaps also the old European admiration for this ancient culture was not then quite extinguished. The

American ideal could therefore be presented to China not simply as uplift but also as an act of anticolonial faith.

One catches the note of the American ideal in the speech made by Anson Burlingame in New York in 1868. Burlingame had served as American Minister in China and offered to lead a Chinese mission to the United States to arouse American interest in China's condition:

> What have you to say to her? She comes with no menace on her lips. She comes with the great doctrine of Confucius uttered two thousand three hundred years ago. She wishes no war; she asks of you not to interfere in her internal affairs.

After claiming that there was nowhere on earth where greater progress had been made in the last few years than in the Empire of China, and insisting that no coercion should be used against China, Burlingame went on:

> She tells you that she is ready to take upon her ancient civilization the graft of your civilization. She tells you that she is willing to trade with you, to buy of you, to sell to you, to help you strike off the shackles of trade. She invites your merchants, she invites your missionaries. She tells the latter to plant the shining cross on every hill and in every valley.*

Despite his sanguine appeal, Burlingame seems to have sensed the real Chinese attitude to the western world in remarking that "she is willing to give you what she thinks is her intellectual civilization in exchange for your material civilization." The guests at the banquet may have overlooked this pointed distinction while ready to be enthused by Burlingame's peroration about China com-

* Quoted in Harley Farnsworth MacNair (ed.), *Modern Chinese History: Selected Readings* (Shanghai: Commercial Press, 1923).

ing out of her proud seclusion. "The imagination kindles at the future which may be, and which will be, if you will be fair and just to China."

Four years after Burlingame's mission, Yung Wing, a Chinese who had been taken to America to study by a missionary, and who graduated from Yale in 1854, persuaded the Chinese government to send the first batch of Chinese students to America. From 1872 to 1875 a hundred and twenty of them went, and although the growth was uneven by 1910 there were over five hundred studying; by 1920 there were over two thousand, reaching a peak of over five thousand immediately after the Second World War. Matching this flow of Chinese to America was the flow of Americans to China. China had been "opened up" to missionary endeavor by unwilling Chinese concessions in 1860. Toward the end of the century, spurred on by the evangelical movement, the call to China became impelling. A modern American historian sees this movement as "the religious counterpart of the new political forces that were stirring men's souls. The new generation of Americans was looking outward, and it was the young converts who directed Moody's revival campaigns from the goal of saving America to saving the world. Mott, Speer, and Eddy were contemporaries of the businessman with an eye to foreign markets and of the new statesman with an irrepressible urge to cast the weight of American influence onto the scales of international power politics. All felt the lure of playing life's role on the world's stage."

And so the seeds were sown. It was China that mattered; China that insensibly became the unstated object of American ambitions; China on which Americans could fasten their ideals. Not that Americans escaped altogether the methods of imperialism in the Pacific. The chance of the Spanish-American War brought the Philippines as an unlooked-for prize in 1898. But the Philippines were regarded simply as a base from which the great China enterprise could be promoted. By that time the missionaries had begun to pour in, the teachers arrived to set up secondary schools and found Christian universities, the engineers charted the prospects, the doctors healed the sick and taught Western medicine. While all this was done by others too—Britain, France, Belgium, and other Europeans—it was the Americans who were the most numerous, and the Americans, unlike the rest, were not at the same time doing these same things all over the Asian and African continents where the European empires stretched. The American effort and the growing American sentiment were much more concentrated on this single, vast country. In an age that believed in progress America needed ground to till.

Perhaps the American attitude is best summed up by John Fairbank, the leading American specialist in modern Chinese history:

> Our traditional China policy resulted partly from attitudes of mind created in us by our westward expansion across the open spaces of the American continent. . . . In the 1890's after the passing of the frontier at home, we established a new theoretical frontier in the Open Door doctrine in China; we were continuing the same process . . . instead of open spaces and natural resources we found Cathay. This new and strange type of human society aroused our curiosity and eventually our sympathy quite as much as our greed or avarice. Toward it we proceeded to apply attitudes developed at home. These were expansive, adventurous, and acquisitive. They included conceptions of progress, growth, and improvement as the law of life.

The result, suggests Professor Fairbank, was "an expansion of the American people which was not solely economic, religious, or nationalist, but a combination of all of them."

Had all this found expression in government policies the confrontation between China and America might have struck reality much earlier. But it did not because the United States was not merely—as a built-in part of the ideology—anticolonial. In turning its back on Europe the United States had tended to be isolationist and thus the American government was unwilling to commit itself to any direct part. An "open door" not a special relationship with China was all that was asked for. Nevertheless thousands of churches scattered over America supported their missionary in China, children brought to Sunday School their pennies for China; the sum of knowledge and sentiment and hope built up to such a point that the United States had, by the 1920's and 1930's, made of China an undeclared protégé.

CHINA'S RESPONSE

It was exactly during these two decades that the future of China and of China's relations with the United States were being determined. The fall of the Manchu imperial house, and with them the system that had governed China on and off for two thousand years, was only one point in a continuing crisis. The proclamation of a republic solved nothing. The great crisis of revulsion, in which China's anger at her treatment by the invading West combined with China's shame at her own failure, only surged up in the revolutionary intellectual flowering of 1919. Until then a despairing and defeated China had been ready to try anything, acting with apparent subservience to a Western world from which it freely confessed it would have to learn. It was only in the years after 1919 that the varied but necessary ingredients of China's renewal slowly fell into place.

First was a proud nationalism that had regained its self-assurance and believed that China's renewal need not depend on outside influence but could draw on China's own strength and traditions. Second was a younger generation sufficiently emancipated from the past to throw over its impediments. And third, there was the need for a doctrine that could give direction to China's revolutionary fervor.

Unlike the liberal and democratic political ideas of western Europe, only communism gave China the comprehensive cover—in defining the nature of man and society in ways that could serve for the twentieth century. Confucianism could go once a substitute source of equal authority had been found.

Even then chance played its part. When constitutional reform seemed beyond China's attainment, revolution seemed the only answer. When Confucianism had been rejected, neither "Science" nor "Democracy" quite filled China's revolutionary sails. The need to learn from the West had been admitted, at one point almost in a mood of utter self-abasement. Yet, instinctively, it was felt that the purpose in learning was to outdo or to get even with the West. For that purpose some supra-Western and at the same time anti-Western doctrine would best serve. The example came happily in 1917 when both the revolutionary method that China wanted and the doctrine of Marxism were put to service in Russia. Even then it needed the political genius of a Mao Tse-tung so to transform the imported doctrine that it could be framed in Chinese terms to serve a Chinese purpose.

And so in these two interwar decades the confrontation was getting closer, though still without any real awareness of what could happen. Then came the 1940's and suddenly, within the space of only one decade, the hopes of a century flowered and were dashed. Everything America had longed for was snatched away. The beginning of violent involvement of course was Pearl Harbor. What this unforeseen Japanese attack did was not merely to end American isolationism in any definable form; it brought about what isolationism had so long deferred—an outright alliance between the United States and China. All through the 1930's Japanese aggression against China had quickened American feelings. The seizure of Manchuria, the encroachment wherever Japanese advantage could be seized, ending in the attack of 1937, spurred on American sympathies. And yet appalling disaster was only round the corner: before the decade had ended there, standing on the platform of the T'ien An Men in Peking was the triumphant revolutionary Mao Tse-tung hurling Chinese pride and self-confidence for all the world to take note of. At the very moment that the United States had emerged from the Second World War as an acknowledged world power, a power capable of acting, and expected to play an international role, the most treasured arena for which that action had so long been prepared was brutally and suddenly closed to her.

Here a point of explanation is called for. When American sentiment for China has been traced and its undoubtedly idealistic motives emphasized, it will be asked how Chinese hatred of America should have reached the heights it has. Was it not British troops who set fire to the Imperial Summer Palace in 1860, French troops who helped to loot it, European powers who made the heavier demands on China whenever Chinese anger led to the murder of a foreigner?

The answer here is that China has always considered itself not a nation in the European sense—the nation-state is a Western concept that has still not settled down in the minds of Chinese—but as a culture. It was an absorptive culture that could make anyone part of the Chinese world, living by the Confucian rules, acknowledging the emperor—and what happier state was there? In short, something very like a mirror image of what the American way of life was thought to stand for. Thus, whatever might have been done by Europeans all through the nineteenth century, in this century it was Americans who were infiltrating so many aspects of Chinese life and proposing to China an American-style solution to its problems, a wholesale package of Christianity, democracy, equality, and progress through free enterprise.

To many Chinese this did offer salvation. Many of the students who went to the United States returned to be either consciously or unconsciously upholders of the American ideals of progress. The Christianity itself never had much of a hold. It was alien to Chinese traditions, and the missionaries in China had become the focus of the antiforeign feeling among the uneducated. From the better-educated Chinese there came retorts: one American missionary complained about the young men who came to his church and quoted Herbert Spencer back at him. Nevertheless, during these decades between the wars the Western-educated Chinese thought of themselves as an élite group, though divided, in a traditional Chinese way, into closely knit associations according to the country in which they had studied.

The students who returned from America were much the largest group and much the most self-confident in their westernization, perhaps because they were most conscious of having imbibed a complete outlook. They could regard Christianity as secondary. And thus to those Chinese who stood outside this westernized group and who were deeply rooted in Chinese nationalism, and who from pride instinctively rejected too great a subservience to any foreign country, the threat to China's renewal was felt to come much more from this insidiously pressed package of Americanism than from the less assertive European nations. The influence of Marxism, much more widespread in intellectual circles than the membership of the Communist party in those days would suggest, only strengthened this resistance. As Chairman Mao Tse-tung has put it: "U.S. imperialism laid greater stress than other imperialist countries on activities in the sphere of spiritual aggression." When one doctrine had to be found, communism best served: when one enemy, one source of poison to China's true character had to be named, it was America that became the scapegoat. As the major world power then already embattled against communism, the choice for China, however unjust on the record, was inherent in the ideological standpoint.

This summary of the American involvement with China takes us up to the Second World War. As in so many other parts of the world it was the decisions that were taken in the years immediately following the war that have left their mark ever since. Nowhere was this so true as in East Asia. For the purposes of a postwar occupation, and as a prelude to peace-making, Korea was divided, with the Russians as the occupying force in the north and the Americans in the south, quickly becoming a cold war division that predated the acknowledged cold war in Europe. That division led to one war and may yet lead to more trouble. The same division was imposed on Vietnam between the Chinese (Nationalists) in the north and the British in the south. Here Roosevelt's firm anticolonialism foresaw and actively sought a liberated Vietnam. Ironically, it was Roosevelt who was ready to sanction American aid to the growing guerrilla force of the Vietminh, while set against this was de Gaulle's faith in France, demanding the return of French rule to expunge the Japanese defeat in the loss of Indochina.

No such conditions applied to China. In China the division was not a postwar product: it was already there. It had been there ever since 1927, and no one believed that the Communists and the Nationalists were going to compose their differences merely because Japan had been defeated. Yet it was to China that American hopes had attached themselves, and it was in China and over China that the postwar United States, at last fully operative on the world stage, got drawn in to an undeclared war.

THE CRUCIAL YEARS

The origins of the war between the United States and East Asia, which now so fruitlessly and tragically goes on in Vietnam, will thus be found in the years between 1945 and 1950. In the months after the end of World War II, Nationalist-Communist rivalry was leading inevitably to resumed civil war in China. Truman, "anxious for the unification of China by peaceful democratic methods," sent General Marshall on a mission of

MAP 3. The American military presence in East Asia. American power defends South Vietnam against the Communist north; South Korea against the Communist north; Taiwan against the Chinese Communist mainland.

Some of this American force is deployed against the threat of China. The Vietnam war has brought a large American land force to Vietnam and air bases to Thailand. The American Seventh Fleet is the most powerfully armed mobile force in the world.

mediation. Through intransigence greater on balance on the Nationalist side than on the Communist—and not for the last time in American relations with the East Asian anti-Communist governments it has been supporting—no successful agreement was reached. The civil war began again in the spring of 1946, and General Marshall left, his mission a failure, in the summer.

Despite lost chances of a coalition government in China, American hopes of some kind of effective relations with the Communists still survived, even though Communist hostility had sharply increased after the failure of General Marshall's mission. American support for the Nationalists by a military mission, weapons, and supplies was kept up throughout the civil war but with less and less hope for any success. At least the catastrophe of trying to "save" part of China by full-scale American intervention (as now in Vietnam) was avoided. Reporting in November, 1948, General Barr, head of the military mission, castigated the failings of the Nationalists, finding a "complete loss of will to fight."

In the same year that the Chinese civil war ended with the outright victory of the Communists on the mainland, Europe had been alerted by Stalin to the necessity of united resistance. This was the beginning of the cold war. NATO came into being. America was committed to an ideological struggle. The conflict with China did not take shape quite so simply. It is, of course, a struggle against communism; but it became and still is more than that: it is a struggle against the men at the head of the Chinese government who have disappointed the United States, who have snatched away American hopes, and who have turned on to the United States a hatred much more venomous and painful than anything the Americans have felt from Russia.

On October 1, 1949, the Communists proclaimed their People's Republic of China. On January 6, 1950, Britain recognized this new government. At that time the Americans had been so bitterly disappointed by the failure of the Nationalists, and were so reluctant to cut off their relations with China simply because it had taken a Communist label, that they, too, were almost ready to follow the British lead and accept a reality that they had no power to change. In his statement on January 5, 1950, President Truman disclaimed any intention of becoming involved in China's civil war, meaning that the United States would not intervene to prevent a Chinese Communist attack on Chiang Kai-shek's retreat in Formosa. From this it followed that only one government of China was envisaged, and that such hopes as existed of American relations with the new China rested on what could be done with that government. There was in any case a sense of curiosity. How would these Chinese Communists turn out? Might they not be willing to coexist with the Western world?

Several Communist actions against American consuls (who had not then been withdrawn from China) soon marred these prospects. China's insistence on Britain sending a mission to "negotiate" diplomatic relations after the announcement of British recognition on January 6, 1950, did not help either. But the real turning point was the North Korean attack on South Korea in June, 1950. And this was followed by President Truman's action interposing an American fleet between the People's government and Chiang Kai-shek's Nationalist government in retreat in Formosa. Though it may not have been thought of as such, this effectively meant American intervention in the Chinese civil war, preventing the Communist forces from liberating the last remaining piece of Chinese territory on which the defeated Chiang Kai-shek had taken refuge, was to be the most fateful action in determining much that has followed.

Then came Chinese intervention in the Korean war itself, so that the most hard-fought battles of the war, heavy in American casualties, were between the Chinese and American armies. All hope of relations with China were jettisoned. But this was not just a decision of state. American sentiment seemed to be picking up again after having been stunned by the speed of the Communist success on the mainland. By 1951, after American soldiers had been fighting the Chinese in Korea, a very different attitude to China's new government was common in official circles and in America generally there was a common sense of chagrin and outrage. Indeed, on both sides of the Pacific the emotions were by now unrestrained.

Somehow this government of China loomed up in the American mind as a nightmare that had to end; it was an appalling accident that had to be corrected; it was something that had been imposed on China; it was unfair, unjust, unrepresentative.

As one American put it in 1951:

> We do not recognize the authorities in Peiping for what they pretend to be. The Peiping régime may be a colonial Russian government—a slavonic Manchukuo on a larger scale. It is not the government of China. It does not pass the first test. It is not Chinese. It is not entitled to speak for China in the community of nations.

Dulles? No—Mr. Dean Rusk.

3

What the Americans Are up Against

OVER A CENTURY, from about 1850 to 1950, the confrontation of America and East Asia had been brought about. The growth of American interest in China, and the readiness of the United States to help China transform herself in pursuit of progress and plenty, reached its apogee with Pearl Harbor: Japan, the East Asian country that had made its own progress and attained its own plenty single-handed, by that attack brought America into an alliance with China. The alliance between the two could then become an international fact and not simply a national sentiment; the full force of American idealism could thus be put to work. Not forthwith, while the war lasted, but in the postwar era of peace and progress. And yet before the decade was out the Americans found themselves vilified as the worst enemy of China's new government. Almost simultaneously two forces that had been taking shape for at least half a century found themselves opposed to one another: the United States as a fully fledged ideological world power and China in the flush of a revolutionary national renewal. These two forces faced each other.

Since 1949 this conflict while never directed militarily against the Chinese mainland has shifted from one point to another: Korea, Formosa, Vietnam. Everywhere the ideological content has been the same. It is true that in Korea the war was fought under a United Nations flag and America had many allies, Britain included, but that does not alter the ideological character of the war I am describing nor should it confuse us over the role played by the United States. The intervention in Korea was an American intervention for American reasons, but under the U.N. flag the Americans felt that their ideological purpose was more firmly upheld. This same American wish is present in Vietnam where the Americans would like to have the British and others by their side, not for any urgent military need of the odd battalion that might thus be added to their strength but to give them the assurance that the righteous purpose of the "free world" was confirmed by being a shared purpose. The crusade needs followers; if it does not have them could they then not merely be apathetic but hostile? He that is not with me is against me is the pit of blindness into which all ideologists are liable to fall.

For this American view of the world Mr. Dulles remains the archetypal figure. His was the policy of a crusade against communism and his was the most typical American sentiment over China. In a sense Mr. Dulles was at war with China's Communist government even though at no point has this conflict become a direct war between these two; only in the Chinese commitment in Korea did the Americans find themselves fighting

Chinese. An American embargo on trade with China was imposed during the Korean war and has never yet been rescinded. Is this not a token of unchanging hostility? No one in Britain thinks that our embargo against Mr. Smith's régime in Rhodesia is anything but a hostile act, aimed at his overthrow or applying a pressure that will force him to change his policy. It was not just the necessities of the Korean war that brought this embargo into force against China. In America the same motives as Britain applies to Rhodesia were at work.

Yet the signs of this war survive to this day, despite the changed attitude that began with President Kennedy and the pained expression of reasonable men in the State Department who nowadays protest that it is not the United States that is being unreasonable or even unpleasant toward China, it is the Chinese who make any kind of dialogue impossible. Quite true. Indeed, ever since 1949 the Chinese have been very difficult as the British have discovered. The world—and not just the United States—will probably find China difficult for a long time yet. In finding fault with the United States, or rather in pointing to American behavior as evidence of hostility I would not wish to falsify the balance sheet. But my theme is the peculiar character of East Asian civilization, the involvement of the United States with this civilization, and the character of the conflict between them as being both ideological and—in respect of China—moved by a sentiment which is the product of a disappointed love.

To a younger generation of Americans this sentiment toward China may already be evaporating. As the United States passes from its first to its second generation in the status of a world power, China is bound to settle into position as only part, though a large and important part, of the world as seen from Washington. Nevertheless, the conflict I am describing has been brought about, and is today still being conducted, by men who uphold both the American ideological role as opponents of communism and in whose hearts beats the feeling that gives a special character to this ideological struggle with China.

There is much evidence to show that this relationship with China has been a special relationship. Have American diplomats found themselves discharged from the service for taking the wrong view of Russia? Have American scholars been attacked for holding a wrong opinion of Stalin? How else can one explain the American reaction all through the nineteen-fifties and even today to a country which having previously recognized the Nationalist government of Chiang Kai-shek proposes to transfer its dealings to the government in Peking of Mao Tse-tung? If one looks at the American record in the annual debate over the Chinese seat in the United Nations, it is impossible to regard it simply as a question of national interest on the part of the United States; there is at the root of it a deep sense of outrage that such a government of China should be acknowledged by the world.

Indeed, one might ask why China at all is one of the five permanent members of the Security Council. It did not seem obvious why China should be so when the future U.N. was under consideration, though it may seem understandable enough now. There is Churchill's astonishment in a wartime visit to Washington where he found "the extraordinary significance of China in American minds, even at the top, strangely out of proportion. . . . I was conscious," he writes, "of a standard of values which accorded China almost an equal fighting power with the British Empire, and rated the Chinese armies as a factor to be mentioned in the same breath as the armies of Russia."

I define the involvement of the United States with East Asian civilization as an ideological struggle in which both participants take the same view of ideology. There is no reason, therefore, to suggest that the wars in which the United States has become involved are all part of one war; still less that they have the same origin on either side. On the contrary, the war fought in Korea and the war now fought in Vietnam have different origins, and the grounds for American intervention may be assessed differently in each case. Far from regarding the Communist forces of East Asia as monolithic, I would insist that each of these Communist movements must be looked at—like all the world's Communist movements—in its own setting and with its own aims.

On the other hand the Americans do not simply find themselves up against the same kind of ideological tenacity in each case. It is also true that at the time when the Americans intervened in Korea and at the time when they were drawn into the Vietnam war the assumption prevalent in American official thinking was that China was behind what was happening, and that by intervening it was Chinese power and Chinese ambitions that were being restrained.

General Gavin, chief of plans in the American army in 1954, has described how at the time of Dien Bien Phu there was even talk in the Pentagon of using one or two nuclear weapons. "We assumed that Peking was a pawn of Moscow," he goes on, "that Russia, thwarted in Europe by NATO and the Marshall Plan was on the march in Asia. The Communist world was assumed to be an integrated monolithic block." Any ideas to the contrary, General Gavin recalls, were regarded as "near-heresy."

The attitude to the Chinese mainland at that time may be deduced from another revelation in General Gavin's article. Admiral Radford, then American chief of staff, strongly favored landing a force in the Hanoi-Haiphong area to counteract the assault on Dien Bien Phu. The air and naval chiefs of staff supported him, but the navy stipulated that they would be unwilling to risk ships in the Haiphong area without first taking the Chinese island of Hainan.

Another piece of evidence was Mr. Walter Robertson's view that the Vietminh had sold their country to Peking, though Mr. Robertson, secretary for Far Eastern affairs in the State Department for most of the relevant period, might be regarded as the model of everything that I am describing in the depth of his emotions over a China that was ruled by Communists.

That these assumptions have since been revised has not lessened the involvement of the United States in the whole East Asian zone, or meant that any peaceful solution has been conceded in Vietnam, or encouraged any more willingness to risk unification in either Korea or Vietnam while any possibility of a Communist régime ruling the whole country is still probable. In each country the same battle to preserve a non-Communist government to contest the claims of the Communist one is part of the logic of intervention. In this sense of the East Asian political context, common to all three conflicts, is the war one.

Having described those features that are common to the American involvement with China, Korea, and Vietnam seen from the East Asian side, it should also be asked how far American purposes in all three cases of her involvement are also essentially one. There is the global strategic argument by which Chinese expansion has to be contained. When this was first put forward the argument rested on Communist expansion because such expansion was thought to be inherent in Communist motives anywhere; since then it is regarded as immaterial whether the motive for expansion is credited to China's communism or to her innate instincts as a potential great power. "Fundamentally we are fighting this war to stop a Chinese attack on Australia," said a senior American official in Saigon to me two years ago. The implication was that Vietnam in itself was not so important: what mattered was the consequences of a Communist victory in Vietnam, or in other parts of Asia, and even, it seemed, as far away as Australia, should Vietnam be "lost." The same argument appeared at the time of the Korean war, but then it was Japan that would be under threat unless a stand were made in Korea.

DOMINO ILLUSIONS

While this argument has lately tended to discount the ideological element and to concentrate on the global confrontation of power—especially since China began to acquire her own nuclear weapons—it needs to be examined at its source. This rests on what has been called the "domino theory," though one might question, for all his virtues, whether General Eisenhower thought he was propounding anything so considered as a theory in the remarks he made at a press conference on April 7, 1954.

He was discussing Dien Bien Phu and the need to defend it (it fell one month later) and explained: "You have a row of dominoes set up and you knock over the first one and what will happen to the last one is the certainty that it will go over very quickly. So you have the beginning of a disintegration that would have the most profound influences."

It is curious that this argument should have survived as long as it has and have seemed credible even to some otherwise intelligent men. It is, if anything, an argument by contiguity. When one country falls under Communist rule then the possibility that the adjoining country will become Communist becomes a certainty—and so the losses proceed to the point where a Communist Australia puts beyond any further doubt the awful and inescapable political fate of New Zealand. A secondary implication on which the first rests is that every country that falls under Communist rule thereby becomes part of an existing monolithic Communist bloc whose cumulative weight of which is put behind the push to overcome the next victim.

At the time General Eisenhower spoke in 1954 it is possible that at the back of his mind was the impression that China's Communist government was a product of Soviet Russian action: we have seen in what colors Mr. Dean Rusk, in 1951 an official of the State Department, saw the government that had been installed in Peking. And it would be natural for General Eisenhower to assume, if he had not followed in detail the history of Vietnam from the formation of the Vietminh in 1941 until the arrival of the Chinese Communist armies, at the end of 1949 on China's southern borders, that the Vietnamese Communist movement was no less a product of Chinese subversion and direction. From such precedents it would have been natural to see the line of dominoes stretching out to the antipodes or in any other of the directions where students with an apocalyptic view of world affairs chose to bemuse themselves by drawing maps with fat red arrows.

Equally it had been a general assumption in 1949 that even if the Chinese Communists had come to power by their own efforts—rather than in spite of the Russians—the alliance signed between the two countries in 1950 was also an alliance to further Communist purpose in the world, that is for the expansion of this monolithic Communist bloc. In fact, both of these assumptions were false at the time and are now abundantly shown to be false. The Communists in China came to power not merely in spite of the Russians; it can furthermore be argued that at no time in their first decade of power were they even close allies of the Russians in the furthering of Communist activity in other countries. There is almost no evidence to support, and much evidence to dispute, the view that China was a party with the Russians to what happened in Korea in June, 1950. Nor can it possibly be shown that China was an important factor in the rise to power of the Vietnamese Communists who also, like the Chinese, had their own revolutionary and nationalist purposes and only enjoyed Chinese aid in the last stages of their struggle with France. Whatever China may have done in recent years, in the phase dominated by Mao Tse-tung's battle with the Russians, and in Mao's own elevation to preeminence as a world revolutionary leader, none of the evidence of the 1950's supports the domino argument.

Furthermore, if one looks all over Asia to find any other

Communist movement that has even approached the prospect of power there has only been one: the Indonesian Communist party, and that was far removed from any other center of Communist power during its period of growth. Though favored by Mao Tse-tung because it liked him and his ideas it cannot be shown that China ever contributed much to the strength of the Indonesian Communist party. Since the appalling massacres of late 1965 and 1966, this party has ceased to be of any significance, but whatever its growth could be taken to prove it does not offer any support for the so-called domino theory.

Another argument against this fear of the spread of Communist rule by contiguity is the even more forceful one of the character of a civilization. There are societies in which communism can flourish as I have argued that it does in East Asia; there are others in which it has little or no chance of growth. Hence it is impossible to lay too much stress on the fact that between Vietnam on one side and Cambodia, Laos, and Thailand on the other lies the most important boundary in Asia, the boundary between the distinctive civilization of East Asia and all the varied religions and cultures in the rest of the continent.

AMERICAN EMOTIONS

We have seen how during the late nineteenth century and until World War II American idealistic intentions to bring progress and prosperity to China were formulated. And then China was suddenly and inexplicably "lost." The use of the word is not casual. In accusing the Democrats of having "lost" China, the Republicans were not making a charge that seemed extraordinary. Many people in America did feel that China had been "lost": they certainly felt an immediate sense of loss. And so one sees this theme recurring in all American thinking about East Asian countries. What is not lost must be "saved." South Korea, Formosa (disguised as the Republic of China), South Vietnam must be "saved."

Saved for what, it might be asked. If one scratched for an answer it would be that by preserving an area of political freedom in which American political ideals might thrive the day would eventually come when by entirely peaceful means Communist rule in the rest of these countries might be overthrown. Such an expectation in respect of China has long ago seemed too far-fetched: American hopes are now generally defined as some evolution of the system on the Chinese mainland that will make it less hysterical and more ready to come to terms with the outside world. It is only fair to say that supporters of a return to the mainland by Chiang Kai-shek have been extremists in the American context. Nevertheless, the United States has found itself defending the Nationalist government in its Formosa retreat and has found reasons of state or of ideology for continuing to do so. The least of these arguments could be that democracy and political liberty were being upheld by this government against the day when such ideals could spark the love of liberty in China itself and thus that which was lost would again be saved. Whatever progress has been made in Formosa, it is not toward democracy and political liberty.

But in essence the ideological view of American purpose does seek something like this in Formosa and South Korea and South Vietnam. They are a part of the "free world." The governments that exist may not be democratic but that is not for want of an American wish that they should be so. Much American pressure was applied in Vietnam to establish constitutional government and run fair elections. No one can doubt the strong urge behind American political purposes in these countries—and they may emerge in Formosa, too, when conditions are more favorable. And indeed it would be hard to rest the case for the war that is being fought in Vietnam, with all that it has meant in suffering for the ordinary Vietnamese, solely on containment in the form of buttressing dominoes, lest Australia and New Zealand fall. The end of the war for the Vietnamese is no less a worthy goal: the survival of democratic and progressive government in which all men are equal.

Seen from the Western distance this is a clinching argument. Is the American motive not admirable? How, it is asked, can Europeans, albeit not as ideologically committed as are the Americans, not share the purposes for which America is fighting? The answer is that they should and would if the American aims bore any relation to the facts. The trouble, the ghastly trouble, is that they do not.

EAST ASIAN PSYCHOLOGY

The point I have been making about the doctrinal character of East Asian civilization needs clarifying and expanding. There is an enduring psychological character in this civilization that survives not merely in China but in these two historical neighbors, Korea and Vietnam, whose civilization derives from China. This is a civilization that has evolved in this one area of the world for over two thousand years. Like it or not its character differs profoundly from civilizations elsewhere. Unlike the rest of Asia or Africa or Latin America it has conserved itself from all but the superficial imprint of Western civilization and, save for Vietnam, from any direct European imperial rule. Most important are the political habits and ways of thinking that derive from the East Asian past. If this nature of East Asia as it applies to Vietnam is not understood for what it is, this war will indeed go floundering on for thirty years and more, with an ever more exasperated United States anguished by its failure, when in its own eyes its motives seem so impeccable.

In China, in Korea, and in Vietnam communism now runs in the grooves made by Confucianism. This new doctrine about the nature of man and the proper organization of society has been brought in to displace the old doctrine. Like the old doctrine, the new one is this-worldly, not other-worldly. The loyalties demanded are different but not so different: it is not surprising that Mao Tse-tung's preeminence should be inflated in China as if he were the emperor of a newly founded dynasty. Thus the new governments proclaim the same righteous moral conviction as they did in the past and exact the same loyalty because the loyalty is due to righteousness. To East Asian thinking, doctrine is central: doctrine and government are inseparable. There is no church to dispute with the state the guardianship of a moral code. And from this organization of the state it follows that there can be only one true government upholding one true doctrine. Of course, popular attitudes in these countries have been influenced by Western ideas: the old rigidities of a Confucian-supported imperial system have not survived untouched. Yet the instincts are still there in all these countries, and those who would follow successful policies cannot afford to ignore them.

Thus it is unavailing to oppose the new doctrinal

forces at work in China, Korea, and Vietnam by governments that have no banner to march under but an empty anticommunism. The Western outsider may see these American-backed governments as much less oppressive than the Communist ones to which they are opposed even if they are so obviously corrupt and inefficient. He reads into this condition something that he would instinctively prefer to the conformity of Communist rule. And so, in the chance of keeping out of the way of government, in retaining an area of personal maneuver, these governments may be preferable to many peasants. They are not, therefore, governments that will win loyalty. In East Asian terms they offer no conviction to which the loyalty can attach itself. At best they can only be interim governments until they can be replaced by a government that does command respect.

The military men who run the undemocratic governments in Seoul, Taipei, and Saigon know this or uneasily suspect it. They vary in the extent to which they are themselves part-westernized (and for that reason unlikely to be successful rulers of an East Asian state) or are still operating largely in an East Asian context. Whatever their personal position, and however much they may be irked by American patronage, they think that their Western backers are not fully a party to the context in which they are operating.

This brings us to another of the distinguishing characteristics of East Asian civilization: its relationship with the outside world and its sense of its own identity. It is a self-enclosed civilization that lives behind walls. It has always assumed, or it behaves as if, outsiders cannot see over these walls and understand how the civilization works. The old rules provided only that if outsiders came in they, too, should acknowledge the bond of loyalty to the emperor, which was the minimal requirement of all men; in time a fuller understanding of the doctrine would enable them to become civilized and to accord with the just principles on which the society was based. This was indeed how the officials in Peking believed British merchants should be "managed" when China's defeat in the Opium War of 1840 forced China to open "treaty" ports to foreign trade in Shanghai and elsewhere.

As a self-enclosed civilization East Asians were, therefore, self-concealing in their relations with nonmembers. They present one face to the world and act in one way in their dealings with foreigners; within the family they have their own dialogue and their own ways. The outsider who wants to understand will get no help in doing so; only persistent enquiry will reveal how the wheels turn internally. And it may be added that ever since East Asian countries have come out to live in the world over the last half century or more very little has been written in explanation of the nature of East Asian civilization by East Asians themselves.

The nature of loyalty as a product of Confucian training is also a very important factor. Shared loyalties are a necessity for those working together. This is one thing that makes it difficult for any East Asian to get along with American "advisers" in Vietnam. If they were colonial rulers that would be simple enough. Such an authority imposed by force would get the loyalty that power can exact. Prudence and temporizing are very much virtues in the East Asian system. But as things are the Vietnamese working with Americans—or fighting with them—is either drawn into a common identification, and thereby in some sense is ideologically changing sides, shifting his allegiance to whatever he senses to be the ethos of Americanism; or he remains rooted in his East Asian ways and thus finds cooperation difficult, irritating, and often exasperating. In the first case, by identifying himself with the outsider he becomes estranged from his own culture; in the second he is open to all the force of discontent that finds the American presence destructive of the civilization that he values. This imbalance will be observable in all the relations the United States has had with its East Asian allies: with Chiang Kai-shek, with Syngman Rhee and his successors in Korea, as well as with Ngo Dinh Diem and his successors. The difficulty is that these "free world" anti-Communist governments, while usually headed by withdrawn, independent East Asian types, are staffed by many of the westernized types who identify themselves with Americanism and thus mislead the Americans about the success of their relationship.

Unlike the Asian cultures of South Asia or Southeast Asia, East Asia finds it very difficult if not impossible to form a true mixture, to import Western ideas which coexist with its own traditions; at least politically, where the Confucianist grooves have lasted the longest, this adjustment is very hard to make. The pattern must be predominantly of the one kind or the other: either cultural and political and hence ideological independence, or submission, sometimes one attitude is concealed by the other.

DEMOCRACY IN EAST ASIA

From this it follows that American ideals of democracy make ineffective battering rams to assault the

East Asian walls. In the long term, yes. When East Asia has made all its adjustments, has renewed itself by means of a twentieth-century doctrine, and has found its way to a working relationship with the rest of the world—then democracy is a powerful idea that could seed itself. Until then it will not be easily imported or imposed, certainly not by any of the men who become rulers in any of these countries whether they are Communist or anti-Communist.

Sometimes Westerners hold up their hands in despair at the slim prospects that a civilized political system such as democracy should ever take root in any Asian country. As usual this is an error arising from the assumption that because we call something a continent and give it a name there exists, therefore, an entity "Asia." On the contrary, it does not exist and never has done in the sense that we imagine. Only in recent decades, seeing themselves in the Western mirror, have "Asians" begun to see themselves as Asians, and then it is only the culturally weaker elements, or those most politically estranged by their westernized views, that find this role congenial, for lack of any deeper cultural roots of their own.

In saying that democracy is wholly alien to East Asian traditions I do not for a moment detract from its chances elsewhere in Asia: on the contrary, all over South Asia pressures for greater democracy make themselves felt even if they are suppressed in many countries in the region. But in considering East Asia one must start from the fact that the very idea of an individual identity and of individual choice cuts right across the loyalties within the group that are one of the foundations of Confucian social structure. Men are not *alone* in East Asia; they are not encouraged to think of themselves as single individuals; they do not act singly but in a group. The whole conditioning of Confucian values is to inculcate loyalties in return for which security is provided. It is impossible to think of such a society as an electorate. There is no such thing in this context, there is only the agonizing choice when rival loyalties present themselves. The East Asian voter is a species not yet evolved, which is not to say that preferences are not to be found between one condition of hardship and misrule and another, or between one general and another in Saigon; I mean only that the election of a government expressing popular choice by an accumulation of individual choices is wholly foreign to the way the society works.

One could go on elaborating this point and discovering in which corners of East Asian society change is visibly at work. It might be said that enough of Western ideas has percolated into the major cities for the beginnings of democratic choice to be observable; nevertheless, the democrat who goes by numbers must admit that this is only a tiny minority. (It might be added in parentheses that it is a pity that the Western world should have attained the quite natural flowering of universal suffrage and consequently has not thought of introducing a limited suffrage in those Asian States in which democracy was established before independence. Still more recently independent rulers never thought to run their country on a limited suffrage that might have avoided a good deal of political corruption.)

This brings me to the conclusion that American purposes in the East Asian context are unlikely to be achieved. In all three of these countries a doctrinal government is in power and claims to be the only righteous government of the country, backing this claim by the accepted and traditional attitude to doctrine. And it is these governments on the Chinese mainland, in North Korea and in North Vietnam that seek to unify the whole country out of both nationalist and Communist conviction. It is the anti-Communist side, backed by the Americans, that refuses to allow any contact between the anti-Communist and Communist parts that might lead to reunification, or talks about its manifest incapacity to reunify the country itself. In so far as these conditions apply to China—with the American-backed Chiang Kai-shek in Formosa; to Korea—with the American-backed Park Chung Hee in South Korea; and to Vietnam—with the American-backed Nguyen Van Thieu in South Vietnam—this ideological war is one war. America faces the same problems and operates in the same political context in all three countries. They are all part of one civilization. And the problem that America faces within this civilization is different in kind from what America faces in any other of her anti-Communist causes elsewhere in the world.

But I have insisted that China is not a dominant power and Korea and Vietnam are not necessarily weak dependencies of their great neighbor. On the contrary, no less under Communist rule as any other rule, the smaller countries are determined to be independent of China and their Communist movements have been so. It remains therefore to consider each case in this tripartite ideological war in which the Americans are involved.

CHINA'S EXAMPLE

There is a dangerous tendency for committed anti-Communists to equate all Communists making no distinction between those of Asia and Europe or those of

East Asia and the rest of Asia. Evil is evil and there is nothing more to be said. Without being drawn off into a byway about the nature of Communist governments it can be said that there are differences that need to be pointed out, differences even within the otherwise common pattern of East Asia. Just as the circumstances of American involvement have been different in the case of China and in the wars of Korea and Vietnam, so the political context in which Communist governments have emerged to lay claim to doctrinal orthodoxy differs in each case. A brief glance at China and Korea and a longer look at the especial complexities of Vietnam is necessary.

As the mother of East Asian civilization China might have been expected to be the most successful and most forceful in its revolutionary renewal by means of doctrine. The history of China from the time of the Taiping Rebellion in the 1850's to the rise to power of Mao Tse-tung in 1949 is one of delay, indecision, and enormous suffering. So great was the chaos that it was a common Western assumption in the early twenties of this century that the Chinese would be incapable of self-renewal: it could only be done by outside aid and, by implication, with the adoption of some outside system, complete with imported Western institutions of a parliamentary kind. The means of her own self-renewal did not seem to exist within Chinese society. Yet China succeeded in finding this strength once it had been sparked into life by a doctrine the Chinese imported themselves rather than had injected into them by foreigners. Even then it is arguable that the very fact that the doctrine had to be imported made of it something distasteful to the proud traditions of East Asia. That it could be done at all was because the doctrine could be presented both as a force for modernizing and at the same time a doctrine that condemned China's invaders as imperialists. And since the alternative doctrines circulating in China were products of these same imperialists, the advantage of Marxism was obvious. Yet by itself these virtues would never have been enough. What Mao Tse-tung did for China was to take Marxism, to add to it many of his own ideals, and to evolve a strategy of revolution within a Chinese context. The doctrines that emerged from the guerrilla experience, unlike the futile urban proletarian violence of the early Russian-dominated years, could give to Chinese communism a moral conviction that could then run freely through the channels once irrigated by Confucianism.

Not that Chiang Kai-shek, already at war with the Communists even before he came to power in 1928 at the head of China's new Nationalist government, attempted in his day to rule without the aid of doctrine. He was much too rooted in Chinese traditions to dispense with it. But all he could do was to present one face to the Western world by adopting Christianity and another to his followers in China by reviving the neo-Confucianism of the nineteenth century, an old doctrine in an old bottle where Mao Tse-tung offered a new doctrine, albeit bottled in the only receptacles available.

Communist success in China depended on many things: on the doctrinal struggle; on the Japanese war and the upsurge of nationalism; not least on the standards of the Communists themselves. Violence and extreme cruelty had been endemic in China both in ordained punishment and in the breakdown of social discipline during a century of revolution. The break with

this tradition of violence which the Communists contrived was—contrary to commonly held opinion in the West—a new start in the experience of the Chinese masses. (Communist psychological pressures are another matter.) And it is fair to conclude that in their appraisal of Chinese communism in Yenan and during the civil war, such qualities, and many other manifestations of dedication to the cause of China's renewal, were enough to bring most of the Western diplomats in Nanking in 1949 to a position of preparing to recognize China's new government. Like the Chinese people they were ready to acknowledge the rough justice of the heavenly mandate. It was not only power that had won.

KOREA

Communism in Korea had no such credentials. Kim Il-sung was as much a protégé of the Russians, put into power by an occupying army, as were the Communist leaders of eastern Europe. In the era of Stalin the government in North Korea looked very much of a piece with Russia's empire in Europe. It seems the Chinese Communists thought so too, judging by the coolness of the relations that existed between the two countries in the year before the outbreak of the Korean war. Only then was an uneasy cooperation forced upon them. Nevertheless the fact that the North Koreans were, as a Communist movement, not a healthy native growth, could not rule out the influences at work. The North Korean Communists were working in an East Asian context: as a government they were exponents of doctrine and doctrine could win support. In their case too the process of adaptation was necessary, though there was no one approaching Mao Tse-tung's caliber to do it. In other ways they were much inferior to the Chinese and still are. Thanks to the effect of the war in Korea and even more to the Sino-Soviet dispute they have nevertheless been squeezed into a position of much greater independence, first of the Russians, and since then of the Chinese, so that now they can make a better national appeal than before. But they are still far from possessing this appeal; their performance during the war did not endear them to the population of the south. And it should be added that the circumstances of the war in 1950, which seemed to reproduce in Korea the opportunism that Stalin had tried in eastern Europe, went a long way toward justifying the intervention on which the Americans decided. But will a government in South Korea, lacking any doctrine but anticommunism, be able to win the loyalties of Koreans merely by economic success? That is the question posed in this corner of East Asia.

The attempt in this essay to set the involvement of the United States in this area in a cultural framework is necessarily done in broad strokes. Many subsidiary factors are ignored. Nevertheless the basic argument remains: that the civilization with which America has got itself involved is a politically intractable civilization now going through a period of its own renewal and for this reason is likely to be unresponsive to outside direction. Its East Asian character will, at least for the period of this renewal, determine its nature. It is carrying out a task that it can only do for itself. Most certainly this is true of China. Probably it is true of Korea. How far is it true of Vietnam? The answer may be the same but for many reasons Vietnam demands qualifications which one can ignore in Korea or China. It is for one thing a frontier zone of East Asia. Unlike the island power Japan, unlike the peninsula Korea backed by China and brought under Japanese rule, unlike the vast and self-confident Middle Kingdom of China itself, Vietnam has been subject to other influences and faces particular problems. We must briefly glance at them.

VIETNAM

Very early in its history the rough territorial boundaries of China had been set. Geography alone did much to keep China within them. Even more the Korean peninsula defined a territory, its land border confined to China, its East Asian parent culture. Vietnam, on the other hand, was something of an overspill. For the first thousand years of its recorded history—and indeed it is the reason why that history was duly recorded—Vietnam was under Chinese rule. When this rule came to an end after the weakening of the T'ang dynasty, Vietnam emerged in 939 independent of China, a situation which ever since it has zealously guarded. On several subsequent occasions the Chinese tried to reassert their authority: once, between 1407 and 1428 holding on for twenty years. Yet having kept China at arms length, the Vietnamese nevertheless acknowledged their tributary status and enjoyed the privilege of their rulers being given the stamp of authority by the Chinese emperor.

Until the early thirteenth century Vietnam occupied a territory stretching not far south of the Red River delta or modern Tongking. To the south lay the Hinduized kingdoms of Champa and Khmer (Cambodia). Both these were weakening: Vietnam was gaining strength in its confident independence of China. By the middle

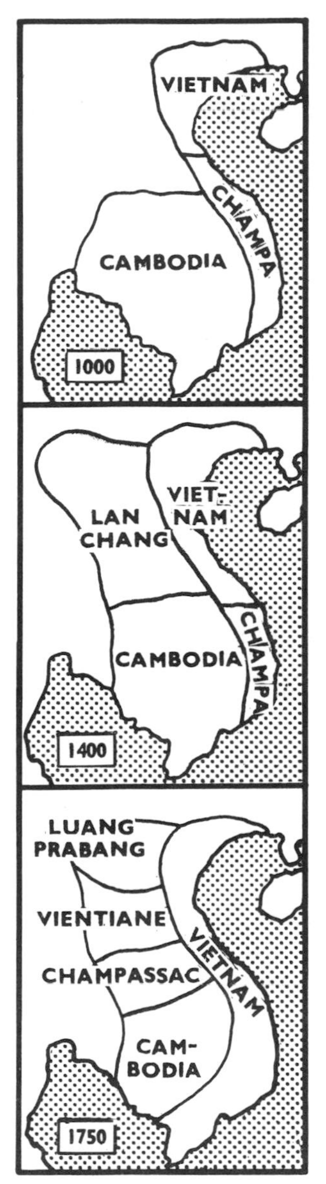

MAP 4. The Expansion of Vietnam. Vietnamese history explains a good deal about the warfare that has been going on for the past twenty years and more. For the thousand years during which it was ruled by China, Vietnam was a much smaller territory covering the modern Tongking. Hence the stronger traditions that govern this part of the country and make northerners tougher and culturally better rooted than southerners. At the time of the top map Cambodia was still a major power and emigration of Thais from southwest China into what is now Thailand was only just beginning.

From 1400 onward Vietnamese expansion southward eroded and finally obliterated the kingdom of Champa (where Hindu influence survived) and eventually came into competition with the equally aggressive and growing power of Thailand. The sufferer in these pressures was the declining kingdom of Cambodia. Adjoining Vietnam to the north was the kingdom of Lan Chang, also the product of Thai emigration. By the end of the seventeenth century this kingdom had lost its unity and divided into three parts. These in turn became subject to Vietnamese and Thai competition for influence. Luang Prabang tended toward Vietnamese protection, Vientiane and Champassac toward Thailand.

It will be seen that Vietnamese settlement in the Mekong delta, where the majority of the South Vietnamese population now lives, is relatively recent and mixed with a strong Cambodian (Khmer) element.

of the fourteenth century Vietnam's southward expansion had gone down the narrow coastal plain almost to the point of the present boundary between North and South Vietnam. As Vietnamese energy and aggression were pursued, by the end of the fifteenth century the kingdom of Champa had all but ceased to exist; Vietnamese power began to touch on the boundaries of Cambodia (then stretching eastward and including all of the Mekong delta). So it continued slowly. By 1700 Vietnamese infiltration into this delta was steadily pushing out or conquering its original Cambodian inhabitants (see map on p. 63). By 1750 the Vietnamese had pushed right across the delta, overcoming the Cambodians to about the point where the present boundary between the two countries lies. At the same time that this was going on in the east Cambodia was suffering encroachment from the west by the Thais, so much so that the much reduced Cambodian kingdom found itself in the eighteenth century forced to pay tribute both to Thai and Vietnamese rulers.

Similar pressures from Vietnam on one side and Thailand on the other also forced the three kingdoms into which Laos was divided to give their allegiance and pay tribute to one or other of these more active powers that abutted on to their territory, but in this case the Vietnamese pressure did not mean much territorial loss nor was it accompanied by new Vietnamese settlement; mountainous Laos had no appeal to rice-growing plain dwellers.

The result of this southward move over four centuries has meant that what is now South Vietnam, and especially the thickly populated Mekong delta zone, is ethnically much more mixed than is North Vietnam.

Chams survived in the south and were intermixed in the population. Khmers (Cambodians) were overrun and still remain in South Vietnam to the extent of over half a million. Here, too, intermarriage brought more ethnic diffusion. Besides this ethnic aspect of South Vietnam as a fringe area there is also the religious confrontation coming at this point of two vast arcs of Buddhist development. From its original home in India Buddhism was exported in one arc that swung right across central Asia into China and from there moved into Japan and into the other East Asian territories. Profoundly molded by its adaptation to East Asian patterns this Buddhism—known as Mahayana—had its part in Vietnamese culture as in Chinese. The other great arc of Buddhism went from India to Ceylon and from there to Burma, Thailand, Laos, and Cambodia, a Buddhism that has enjoyed a ubiquitous role in the society of all these countries and still dominates village life. This is the Hinayana or Theravada. The Khmers were Theravada Buddhists, and those who were overrun by Vietnamese conquest have remained so within the confines of South Vietnam.

Furthermore, the Vietnamese push southward was paralleled by a split in the ruling authority. From the sixteenth century until the end of the eighteenth Vietnam remained divided by dynastic quarrels. Thus, throughout the period of southward expansion into what has become South Vietnam, a different ruler held authority in the South from the North. And when the reunification did finally come under Gia Long in 1802 he was an emperor backed by the French who were by that time steadily increasing their interest in the country (in which French missionaries had been active for over a

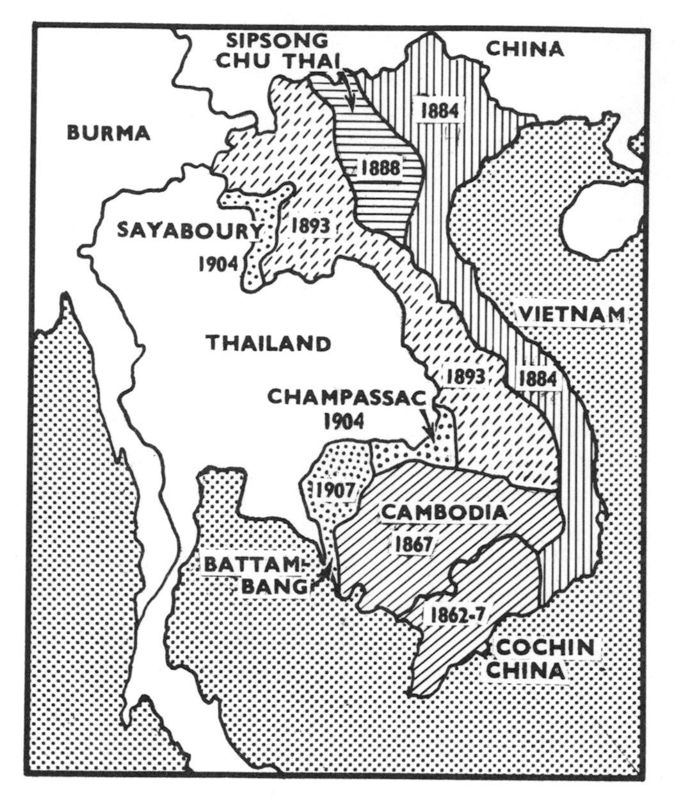

MAP 5. French Power in Southeast Asia. (The variably shaded areas show French penetration chronologically.) The power conflict between Vietnam and Thailand over the weaker states between them was made more complicated by the intrusion of French rule. The dates on the map show when French power was asserted in Cochin China and eventually in all of Vietnam. The protectorate extended over Cambodia did rescue this country from the dominance of both Thailand and Vietnam. Thai resentment at having to disgorge provinces—Battambang, Champassac, Sayaboury—to Cambodia and Laos led to their seizure once again by Thailand when they were allies of the Japanese during the war and France was powerless. After the war France took them back again.

The attitudes of Prince Sihanouk in Cambodia, of Thailand, and of the Vietnamese toward Laos are all affected by this past history even though expressed in Communist, neutralist, or anti-Communist terms.

century). During the nineteenth century French rule was imposed in the south of Vietnam (1860's) and center; in the north only after a war with China in 1884 (see map on p. 66).

This history of Vietnam will have suggested how less stable and less settled South Vietnam is compared with the north; it also follows that historical ambitions of Vietnamese conquest and influence were interrupted and eventually arrested by the power and influence of the French. Such impulses, and the assumptions of superiority that have survived from the past, may now be at work again in the rivalry between Vietnam and Thailand over Laos, for example, and even Cambodia.

To this pattern of confusion that applies peculiarly to this corner of East Asian civilization there must also be added the legacy left by the period of French rule. The protectorate that was established in Cambodia in 1865 (for once a genuine use of the word, since Cambodia might have disappeared entirely under the rival pressures of Vietnamese and Thai power if France had not intervened—a fact that now explains Prince Sihanouk's desperate suspicion of both these powers on his flanks) and then in Laos in 1895, stretched French power across the cultural boundary of East Asia and the Theravada Buddhist kingdoms of Southeast Asia. At a time when this cultural and political boundary was fluid and undergoing change—and would, no doubt, eventually have found a point of balance—French rule confused the issue even more.

The area thus became known as French Indochina (from the nowadays often misused expression Indochina which was then taken to mean all those territories which in European maritime experience lay between the major cultures of India and China), and inevitably its internal boundaries were blurred. Moreover, as was common in imperial rule in this part of Asia, a class of craftsmen, traders, and clerks was necessary, and where the local population failed to provide such skills the rulers turned to immigration. Hence, in this area, apart from the Chinese immigrants who had been present for centuries and now came in even greater number, the French encouraged the Vietnamese to emigrate to Cambodia and Laos where their skills, readiness to work hard, and their intelligence could be put to good use. The result has been that the Vietnamese, given a sense of superiority in any case over these Southeast Asian neighbors, saw themselves as the natural leaders of the anticolonialist nationalism of the whole area ruled by France and not simply of Vietnam itself. Thus the expansive ambitions of the earlier history of Vietnam were reinforced by the colonial period and to this day the Vietnamese see themselves as having ill-defined rights in Laos and Cambodia which both these countries fear are being asserted by the vigorous Communists of North Vietnam. (So, for that matter do the Thais fear the Vietnamese as rivals for these territories—the old struggle is still there below the ideological surface.) It is this Vietnamese interest in Laos and Cambodia, extending even to the fringes of Thailand, which more than anything else gives currency to the domino theory, if one looks at the war in Vietnam without looking back into Vietnamese history.

The outcome of this history has meant that East Asian cultural characteristics and political stability are thus most deeply entrenched in North Vietnam, are fairly strong in the center, and are confused by other ethnic and religious intermixtures in South Vietnam. It is the south that is unstable, filled with pockets of religious or ethnic minorities, capable even of generating its own concocted religions in the twentieth century—Cao Dai and Hoa Hao, both of them growing up almost as warlord-run kingdoms with their own armies.

If circumstances had gone on to make South Vietnam wholly different from the North, even perhaps to domesticate it in the true Southeast Asian zone to which climatically it belongs, it might also have been capable of total independence. But it is not wholly different. It is essentially weaker than the North. Yet it is both Vietnamese in culture and outlook while resenting the toughness by which these qualities in the North are imposed upon the South. One could hardly have chosen worse grounds than South Vietnam to stand on politically.

What makes the American task so much more difficult has also made things harder for the Communists. The movement led by Ho Chi Minh is neither as nationally indigenous as Mao Tse-tung's Chinese party nor as tested by struggle. As it was formed in 1941 the Vietminh was a coalition of nationalist forces dominated by the Communists. In the nationalist forces it cooperated with, and those it opposed (and did away with in various ways including murder when the struggle to take over the country arose in 1945), it was not much less capable of appealing to the sentiment of the people than Mao Tse-tung's party was. Ho Chi Minh had the chance of overriding popular hesitation as Mao Tse-tung did. But what the Vietminh was up against was a much more divided, much less coherent society than China's. If South Vietnam had had the same tough fiber as the

North, the grip of the Vietminh in the southern part of the country might have been such that the French would not have dislodged them so easily as they did there in 1945. As it was, during the war against the French, the Vietminh dye sunk in very deeply in parts (see map on p. 72).

Certainly the Chinese Communist army won the civil war in China as much because it was the first honest, disciplined, and markedly less cruel body of men that the ordinary Chinese had encountered in all their lifetimes. The moral capacities of the movement were manifest. The North Vietnamese have fallen short of these Chinese standards albeit they are still formidable. But there comes a sharp descent in the scale to a movement that is, cold war arguments notwithstanding, South Vietnamese in original organizations and character. The National Liberation Front and its guerrillas have fallen far short of the North Vietnamese standards and have constantly weakened their appeal by crude cruelty and methods of terrorism (grenade tossing in Saigon streets, ruthless killing of Saigon government civil servants as in the Tet offensive of 1968, and murders of picked civilians). All this is behavior of a kind that the Chinese Communists avoided on principle and only occasionally lapsed from in practice during the course of their civil war.

Against the North Vietnamese exponents of doctrine came Ngo Dinh Diem, a man East Asian enough in his sense of tradition to discover for himself a doctrine that should serve his purpose. But the Personalist philosophy of the late Emanual Mounier was too exotic an import from France to mean much even to the educated. Although he was a figure who commanded respect in traditional ways, Ngo Dinh Diem was also too narrow-minded and too ruthless to succeed in running a government that could have a moral appeal enough to rival the north. As a Roman Catholic he could appeal to an element in the population that existed in Vietnam in number and tradition as it did not in any other East Asian country, yet in doing so Diem tended only to side with one element and divide himself from the rear. As a Roman Catholic he was that much less a national figure.

After Diem went in 1963 there has been no power exercised in Saigon by men who could command respect as national figures, possessing even a visible portion of the moral integrity for which the Vietnamese would look in their rulers. Against this it must also be said that the National Liberation Front has failed to attract the support of prominent national figures. Of course, the circumstances have not been the same as in China, and the war fought there is not to be compared with the war in Vietnam. The Chinese intellectuals who flocked to Mao's standard during and after the Japanese war could at least live and work in a liberated area rather than a battered, defoliated jungle. And perhaps China's case had some parallel in the support Ho Chi Minh could garner in 1945. But very little can be said for the intellectual support won over in its own right. At best the N.L.F. is likely to win such support on balance by leading anti-American feeling.

One might legitimately ask the question then: How far does the American involvement in Vietnam reflect the same conditions as elsewhere in East Asia? Alternatively is the case of Vietnam, and especially the particular case of South Vietnam, sufficiently outside the pattern

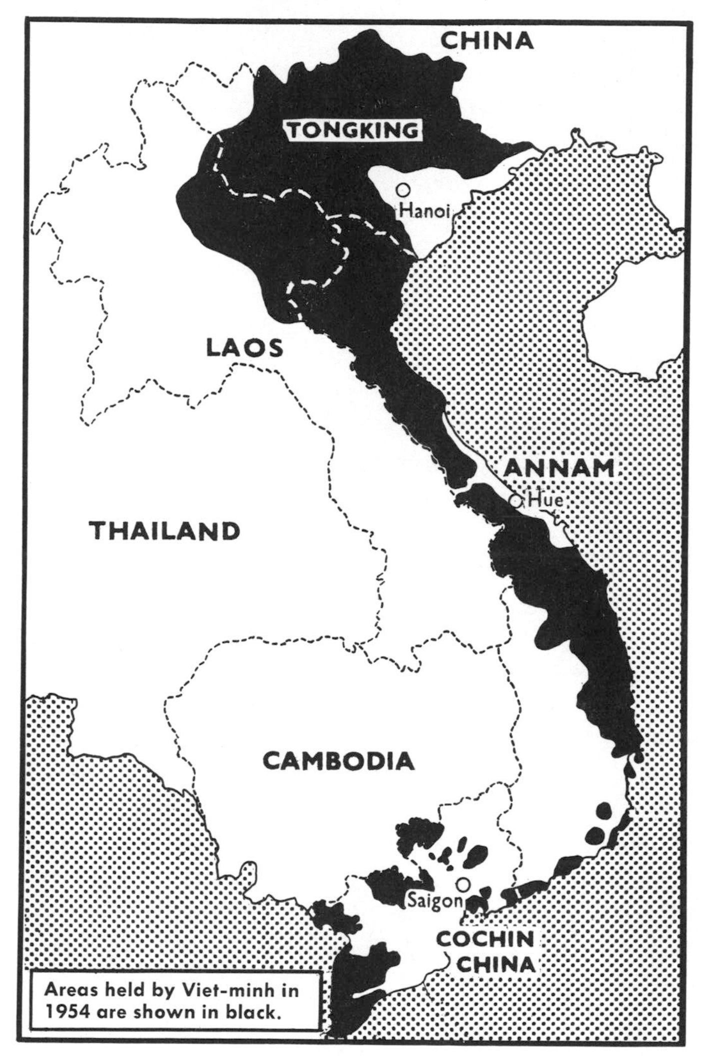

MAP 6. Communism and the war in Vietnam. The Geneva settlement divided Vietnam temporarily at the seventeenth parallel and the fighting forces of each side were withdrawn to the north and the south of the demilitarized zone. Argument about how the war began again often suggests that the Vietminh had left agents in the

I have defined that it should not be included in the arguments I am advancing here? This thought crossed my mind when I first visited Saigon in 1952. If culture could do anything in East Asia then certainly France had done much in Vietnam to inject new cultural patterns. Even today one catches the whiff of Europe about the Communists of Vietnam as one does not catch it among those of China, Korea, or Japan. Indeed, and most ironically, Ho Chi Minh the old Comintern internationalist was enough touched by Western ideas that when he proclaimed his independent government of Vietnam in Hanoi on September 2, 1945, he even included in the document he read out those familiar words, "All men are created equal. They are endowed by their creator with certain inalienable rights; among these are Life, Liberty and the pursuit of Happiness . . ."

I had, as I say, my doubts in Saigon. A Frenchified upper class—though fast disappearing to settle in France—weird religions, a Roman Catholic minority of substance, half a million Theravada Buddhist Khmers, a wholly tropical climate—might not South Vietnam get lopped off and fall into the lush background of Southeast Asia? If this were not the cultural backing given to the Western case for partition made at Geneva in 1954, might that partition nevertheless not work because of

---

south. No doubt they did, but events did not depend solely on them. The Vietminh presence in South Vietnam, though much less strong at all times than in the north, was nevertheless considerable.

This map shows those areas held by the Vietminh at the time when the war was ended by the Geneva settlement. It will be seen that considerable areas of South Vietnam were then, and had been for several years, under direct Vietminh control. It is the population of these areas that has contributed to the strength of the N.L.F. and the most strongly held Vietcong bases are in the same areas in which the Vietminh was strong twenty years ago.

it? Any doubts I had were ended when I went to Hanoi in September, 1954, when the Communists marched in to take over under the Geneva agreement. I had been "liberated" in Shanghai in 1949 and had watched the victory march there, talked to the newcomers, and assessed as best I could the reactions of the people to their new rulers. In Hanoi I did the same, and the pattern was almost identical. All the East Asian character was there. It was plain that the South did not have a separate enough sense of identity to stand up against this. The cohesive force of East Asian traditions working with a new doctrine would be far too powerful, and the force would be quite enough to go on until the day when Vietnam was unified. Anyone, I thought to myself then, who believes that South Vietnam can be "saved" in any political sense for the West does not know what he is up against.

TRANSFORMING THE CONFRONTATION

But there it is. The decisions were taken and by men almost wholly ignorant of the civilization into which they were intruding. What solution can there be now but that America should somehow extricate itself from this mistake? And that does not only mean Vietnam, though that is the most disastrous involvement, which is coming in its distant effects to cripple all hopes everywhere in the world. Sometime disengagement will have to follow in Formosa and in South Korea, though the timing and the solution will be different in each case. By now, in any case, the old emotional commitment of America to China is fading. While this emotional commitment was strong it made of communism in China an enemy of the United States much more vicious than communism elsewhere in the world. Perhaps that is still true of the Dean Rusks and Walter Rostows. A younger generation of Americans has grown up in an America that is a fully functioning world power; China should no longer play the exclusive part in their minds that it did for their parents.

In this essay I have been stressing those characteristics of East Asian civilization which govern its political thinking and run so strongly during its present phase of renewal as a civilization. They are characteristics overlooked in the West, and it is the ignorance of these characteristics which has contributed to this war in Vietnam. Perhaps in insisting on them I risk exaggerating them. I do not mean to imply that democracy is not a possibility in East Asia in the future, or that its Communist system will always be like what we have seen in China this last twenty years or in Korea or in Vietnam.

To prophesy, I would suggest that the historian a century hence may by then be referring to something that would be simply *the* East Asian doctrine, a doctrine molded by time and circumstance and by the powerful traditions still at work among these peoples. There is a humanism within the tradition which can have its effect, but it can only work on the doctrine if the molding process is done by the East Asians themselves. In China that molding is going on: in many ways the reaction to Mao Tse-tung's cultural revolution may have speeded it up. In Korea and Vietnam it remains arrested, the powerholders embattled against an alien enemy.

At many points in this essay I have been making broad generalizations. Having gone so far I might conclude with some more. They are all opinions I had formed after watching communism at work in China, and then seeing something of Vietnam in the early

1950's and comparing these East Asian countries with political life and revolutionary movements in other parts of Southeast and South Asia. Events have not falsified them although fourteen years have passed since then and almost twenty have passed since the Communists swept to power in China. Here they are then:

East Asian communism is adapted for East Asian needs and becomes thereby inherently unexportable. The renewal of its own civilization is China's prime purpose. The Chinese have rarely been successful imperialists. Theirs is not an outgoing civilization but rather an *indrawing* one.

Democracy runs against all East Asian traditions and will not be implanted by outsiders. Only close contact with the rest of the world might, in time, allow it to seed itself.

By contrast an impulse toward democracy exists in all other parts of Asia. If it is inhibited these governments may get the guerrillas they deserve but they will not be successful *as Communists*, however much Chairman Mao cheers them on.

East Asia's relations with the rest of the world will take time. Its present crisis of revulsion against the world —against all the outside world—is a product of a long past. It is a self-contained civilization (living behind Great Walls) capable of fury and aggressive action when denied what it thinks are its rights but it cannot be, in this phase of self-renewal, the expansionist civilization that so many people fear.

Better still, sum it up in four words, badly needing to be understood in London and Paris, in Delhi and Cairo as much as in Washington—East Asia is different.

Index